# COSMIC
# CROSSROAD
# COUNTDOWN

## THE FIG TREE & PERFECT STORM

### DR. PETER HOFMANN

ISBN 978-1-957220-95-6 (paperback)
ISBN 978-1-957220-96-3 (hardcover)
ISBN 978-1-957220-97-0 (digital)

Library of Congress Control Number: 2017911412

The book has been revised as of August 2020, for clarity and ease of comprehension. Prior to the Solar Eclipse of 2017, God gave Dr. Hofmann a message to share with the world. The Countdown began with the 4 Blood Moons, a Solar Eclipse, and then the Great Sign of Revelation. This Divine Cosmic Countdown continues to this day.

Rushmore Press LLC
1 800 460 9188
www.rushmorepress.com

Printed in the United States of America

# ACKNOWLEDGEMENTS

Pastor Dennis Kavanaugh whose understanding of Genesis, Daniel and Revelation came after much studying and teaching at Dallas Theological Seminary and at his church. We enjoyed his depth of understanding and willingness to investigate with us the deeper meaning and treasures of God's Word. He always gave us a listening ear and a keen eye to see important details and answers from beyond the horizon.

Angie McCutcheon, a good friend, who allowed me to bounce ideas and thoughts around in the courtroom of Biblical Truth. She patiently helped me expand my knowledge and sources.

Other Pastors and ministries including Troy Brewer's preaching on Numerology and John MacArthur's insights on Biblical Truth. Generous thanks to Jonathan Cahn for his ministry on Prophetic history and the fingerprints of God in current events. Also, many thanks to the ministry of Jonathan Cahn, David Jeremiah, Tony Evans, Jimmy Evans, and websites such *The Signs of the End*.

This is just the Beginning- LOOK out for the next book to be out in a few weeks <u>Cosmic Crossroad Countdown: The Invisible War</u>.

# DEDICATION

This book is dedicated to first responders and frontline doctors and nurses who are fighting the invisible forces that are assaulting society and our wellbeing. Included in the wall of strength and fortitude are those who serve on the mission field or in a ministry. My prayer is for each of them as forces of darkness and principalities of wickedness increase their evil intent. The spirit of Jezebel and the anti-Christ will not prevail for He who is in us is greater than he who is in the world.

Ephesians 5, warns us to, *"Walk as children of light learning what is pleasing to the LORD. Be careful how you walk not as the unwise but as wise making most of your time because the days are evil."*

# Reviews

Angie McCuthcheon: *"A Provoking look into the future..."*

T. Williams: *"Thought Provoking, A must read."*

Amazon Reviews:

*"What a Great book, Dr. Hofmann connects Biblical and secular history."*

*Letter to those with Eyes to See:*

*How can so many pastors have so many conflicting viewpoints? Is the Holy Spirit a spirit of division and confusion? How can gifted pastors claim that the Babylon of Revelation must be in the present nation of Iraq? Then we hear most other Prophetic Teachers claim that Babylon cannot be in Iraq but is Rome or New York City or some other existing area? The same is true for Revelation 12. Major speakers claim that it is in chronological order with the rest of Revelation yet when presented with simple scriptural facts they back off. So, what is the problem? They see but do not see, they hear but not hear—much like the Pharisees.*

*Why are most religious leaders afraid to comment on the Sign of Revelation 12 and other prophetic Signs for this Day and Age? Is it because of pride, power, ego, and the dark forces of the spirit of Academia? The Truth will set you free. Four years ago, almost to the day, the Holy Spirit put this message in the Author's heart as his good friend and he shared the Gospel at White Rock Lake with their ministry called "Answers on the Rock." The Lord led them to write this message before the great American Solar Eclipse of 2017. Everything presented was given by God and everything came true. Why then have his books come under spiritual attack and faced a wall of apathy and disinterest? Why has it still been smothered under other people's false predictions? The Sign of Revelation 12 was clear in its message that President Trump was not going to win another election. It was clear that we would come under a massive "invisible attack" that would generate worldwide upheavals and a tsunami of New Beginnings. Five other insights came true as revealed by God's message for the Church.*

*God's Word does not return void. Some claim that other spiritual leaders have been blinded by their prejudices or traditional thinking. What is amazing is that many are blind to their own blindness. Most of the Baptist-Evangelical community accuses the Presbyterian-Catholic community of being confused when it comes to Eschatology and the belief that the Church has supplanted the Promises made for Israel for the end-time events. They strongly accuse them of being wrong-headed for replacing God's promises to the nation of Israel with His promises for the Church. They accuse Replacement Theology of being ignorant of Theological and Historical facts. And they berate half of Christianity for turning the great Prophetic books of Isaiah, Jeremiah, Ezekiel, and the minor prophets into a collection of symbolic alliterations and metaphors. They denounce these groups for suggesting that there is no literal Millennial kingdom, no rapture, no 2nd Coming with a throne in Jerusalem, and no salvation for the nation of Israel. That's fine but do they have the Whole Truth and nothing but the Truth. Can their arrogance blind them from the simple facts presented in this book?*

*Many are guilty of extreme bias against the facts that stand in their way. 1) They refuse to acknowledge that Revelation 12 is important in the Eschatological timeline. They attacked anyone who suggested the Sign of Revelation 12 had any purpose whatsoever in Prophecy for today. 2) They refuse to see the landscape of the future in Revelation 12 in both the meaning of the "child" and in the very fact that God's Signs point forward and NOT backward in time. 3) They demand that Revelation 12 is in Chronological order with the rest of Revelation, but it is NOT as evidenced by Chapter 7 and the appearance of the tribulation saints in heaven before Satan is cast out of heaven. 4) They rudely discount anyone who has been given a divine role in presenting any message that you feel does not fit your bias. 5) They discount God when He states that this Sign is His Great Sign forewarning this generation of things to come. 6) They discount Science when it clearly proves that this Sign happened and that this Sign had a similar appearance at the Bethlehem Star. 7) They have failed the Church by NOT allowing the warning to go to their members and to the world. For this God demands that they shirk their pride and humbly listen to His Voice and become shepherds of His flock. God is demanding our attention so that we can make Every Effort to Save the Lost and reach all Tribes before it is too late. Sincerely Yours, In His Love, Grace, & Mercy*

# CONTENTS

# CHAPTER ONE

# Introduction

Many pastors and priests do not want to teach nor discuss End-Time events and Prophecy. Many are not trained in that area or do not see prophecy as having any relevancy. Some have even suggested that the Bible discourages the study of the "Signs of the Time." This is far from the truth! The fact is just the opposite is true. The Lord scolded the Pharisees for not knowing the signs of the age: "*When it is evening you say, 'It will be fair weather, for the sky is red'; and in the morning, 'It will be foul weather today, for the sky is red and threatening. Hypocrites! You know how to discern the face of the sky, but you cannot discern the signs of the times*" (Matt. 16:2-3). It is refreshing to know that some past writers broke through this malaise with best sellers like "<u>The Late Great Planet Earth</u>." This should show the leadership of the church that the public is genuinely concerned about the signs of the time and want information on biblical prophecy.

Hopefully, this book will pique your interest and will motivate you to study prophecy and its relationship to our near-term future. Note that Jesus referred to the elements or the atmosphere as the common sign of a coming storm. Was this a subtle warning to the leaders of His time of another storm? These highly educated leaders had missed the greatest Sign of their time, the Bethlehem Star. The meaning of the star was understood by pagan kings of the East who must have committed months to observation and preparation before embarking on a difficult and dangerous journey to Israel. Is this a sign that educated leaders of our time will miss the other Great Sign?

Does the Bible proclaim another astronomical Sign; one for our time as significant as the Bethlehem Star? Jesus did tell His followers to observe the Signs in the Sun, Moon, and Stars, Luke 21:25, and He did reveal the Great Sign of Revelation 12 to John the Apostle on isle of Patmos. John is fondly known as the Apostle who Jesus loved and was present during important events in the ministry of Jesus. He was commanded by Jesus Christ or the Angel of the Lord to write all things shown him concerning the church and future end-time events.

The book will explore a Crossroad involving four pathways of prophecy connecting history and the Fig tree, the prophecy taught by Jesus Christ, the Great Sign of Revelation 12, and the testimonies of both prophets and Apostles along with the testimonies of the city of Jerusalem, the Tabernacle, and Israel's wilderness experience. These puzzle pieces will help us understand the "day" that we are in. Just as the scribes missed the birth of the Savior 2000 years ago, will our dedicated scholars miss a Great Sign warning of His eminent return?

Jesus gave a warning or sign to his listeners and to all those throughout history who see His Message in the Word. Concerning His 2nd Coming He states: *"For as in the days before the flood, they were eating and drinking, marrying, and giving in marriage, until the day that Noah entered the ark, and did not know until the flood came and took them all away, so also will the Coming of the Son of Man be."*

We will see that the Fig Tree is a key to unlock Prophetic Truth spoken by Jesus himself in all 3 Synoptic or Chronological Gospels. The meaning of the Fig Tree is the first piece of the puzzle missed by many Biblical scholars. They believe that the Olive Tree represents Israel, but they fail to note that Isaiah was given a message to the nation that said the olive tree would be cut down with an axe. However, the roots and trunk remained in the garden allowing the nation to come back in the future. In the meantime, the Fig Tree would replace the Olive Tree, providing a covering under which people might find rest and restoration. Therefore, Jesus uses the Fig tree in his prophetic Olivett parable shared in Matt. 24:32.

The birth and death of Jesus changed everything on earth including the earth calendar, the course of empires, and the opening of heaven's door of Salvation to anyone who believes, Jew or Gentile. This new wheel of time introduced a new paradigm centered on Jesus Christ, His promised return, and other climatic events revealed through the prophets and the book of Revelation. This prophetic path is illuminated by the return of the nation of Israel, God's Great Sign in the Stars, the Jubilees with its generational periods, and the Testimonies of people, places, and events. When these pieces fall into place, we will see a divine pattern that will help us understand the Puzzle *of the Ages and whether todays pestilence will continue.*

It is important to note that the Great Sign in Revelation 12 is of special significance because God calls it the "Great Sign" and He places it right in the middle of the most significant prophetic book in the New Testament. This is not an arbitrary sign that can be ignored as it has been by the scholars. Once the sign occurs, a new paradigm, is introduced just as the Bethlehem Star introduced the first coming of Jesus Christ and began a new paradigm. There were no international announcements, no shock waves, and few noticed this new Star or Light, yet a significant event was about to happen.

The book will explain that when the Great Sign happened in 2017 there were other significant stelar signs pointing to it including: Comet P67, the Moon, 2 key stars in the constellations, Jupiter, Mars, Venus and Mercury? So why did God arrange for this to happen 2020 years after the Bethlehem Star? What is the significance and how will it affect us today? As you read on you will understand why we add three biblical Hebrew years to 2017 in order to get the two thousand and twenty years. All the elements that are pointing to the *"Great Sign of the Woman of Revelation 12"* must be studied and understood for it may open a door to a darkness that affects us all. This cosmic orchestration overlaps other key events such as special Hebrew Holy festivals and generational periods. This epic convergence will show that God has an important warning for us today.

We will see that Revelation's Great Sign has a profound message pointing to the threat of invisible forces. As we read on, we must ask: Are some of these dark forces preparing the stage for the Anti-Christ? In the last few years have we witnessed an unusually aggressive spiritual attack on our democracy and on the souls of men, women, and children? Why do we see such a rise in confusion, depression, and suicide? Who or what are these dark forces? Why are we seeing huge uptakes in drugs and pornography? Hacking, cyberattacks, and other invisible forms of warfare have cost our economy billions of dollars. The greatest threat has been a strange invisible virus that is described as zoonotic and possibly engineered from multiple host animals. The virus attack generated tracking, forced vaccinations, and other mechanisms that will help in the anti-Christ control the masses.

Back in early 2017 before the Solar Eclipse, I predicted that this would be a time of personal and national testing followed by a time of *New Beginnings* at every level of society. It coincided with a series of natural disasters, a national conspiracy, and Middle East events. This book will explore a paradigm where God uses numbers and dates related to Jubilee years, prophecy, and Biblical Generations to warn us and guide us. God will draw more and more people to Him as He allows extreme weather and other events to shake up the nations.

We will explore many significant signposts including the testimony of the city of Jerusalem and the Tabernacle. This book will reveal amazing *Number* sequences that appear throughout time and nature. We will clearly see that God is a God of Order. All of this should motivate us to keep a sound mind so that we can pray, learn, and put trust in God's Word, as we look to God for answers and direction. This book is for everyone and not just those who like prophecy or love to pick up a Bible.

Have you used the sun to tell the time of day or used geological formations such as mountains to find a destination? A map is helpful, but you can also take pictures to remind you of mountain peaks or familiar buildings. Likewise, God will use familiar events and structures including the stars to point us to His plan for the ages. Believe it or not the Bible is going to be your best compass and road map to answers concerning the time we live in. Be prepared to open the most popular book in history, the Bible, and study it as you follow along with this book. You will be amazed how God blesses you.

The Book of Revelation says, *"Blessed is the one who reads aloud the words of this prophecy; and blessed are those who hear, and who understand for the time is near."* Prophecy can be difficult to understand and that is why it is important to pray about it and to use many different sources.

Jesus Christ appeared to John the Apostle on the island of Patmos many years after all the other apostles had passed away. He revealed to John future events that have not happened yet. Most of those events would be laid out in chronological order, but some would not. Chapter 12 for instance does not follow that progression. It is obvious that Satan must be kicked out of heaven before the *Wrath of God* begins. Satan must be on earth to cause the necessary chaos and persecution of those who have not taken the Mark of the Beast. He will enter and empower the anti-Christ. We should also note that John was given a first-hand view of the future and had the benefit of the writings of the other disciples, the Prophets, and rest of the Old Testament.

The book of <u>Revelation promises that whoever reads it or hears it will be blessed.</u> It is a perfectly accurate completion of God's Prophetic message. It along with the rest of God's Word has been passed from one generation to the next with Grace, Justice, and Love. God expressly desires to reveal His truth to all of us before He returns. Since I have not had much time to get this book out, I am totally dependent on the Holy Spirit to open doors, hearts, and minds quickly. My prayer is that you prepare yourself with prayer for what will unfold.

Most have seen Michelangelo's famous Sistine Chapel rendition of God's finger touching man. The iconic image has impacted our perception of God. In much the same way, I will take poetic license to illustrate how God is intimately involved in our history and in our lives. Just as God's *finger-touch* is not Biblical, my *Wheels of Time* are not entirely Biblical. God does touch our hearts and everything about us. Likewise, He is the Supreme Timekeeper, who watches over us and prepares events and interventions to help us, as He fulfills prophecy and promises. He is the *Beginning and the End*, and He is the *Same Yesterday, Today and Forever*. And He is in Control of Time, Matter & Space.

As you read this book you will see that I am both an artist and a scientist. You will understand how each works well in explaining and comprehending God's Word. An Artist must visualize his subject, and therefore, must understand it in 3 dimensions to *paint* it: the textual meaning, the visual meaning, and the emotional or spiritual impact. The scientist, however, is trained to observe and comprehend the facts or meanings from various perspectives or conditions, and to objectively reproduce the same result or truth. Accuracy is important and so is evidence. Both observation and visualization will us in this study.

You will see that this is one area that many Bible expositors fail in. They often do not apply logical science or human behavior. I enjoy the challenge of hermeneutics and exegesis especially after having taken two eleven-year Bible studies and a Bible Study Methods course under the great Howard Hendricks. I want the reader to understand the power of God's message in the full light of truth, so it impacts both the heart and the mind. Also, being true to the Spirit brings deep joy and hope. Forty-three years as a doctor, has taught me that logical prevention saves lives. The Truth may not be obvious and is often hidden under layers of dogma or poor logic. Jesus said, "*I AM the Truth, and the Truth will set you Free.*" He removes the fog of bias.

I pray this book will challenge your perspective on Prophecy and that God's inspired Word will set you free.

In Figure 3, four blood moons and the Jewish feast days form a wheel in time that reveals a prophetic 3½ year time template leading up to the end of a prophetic 50-year Jubilee on September 22, and to the *Great Sign of the Woman* on September 23. Later you will see that this was a unique time when planets sun, moon, and constellations convened in a special pattern. Prophecy is of extreme importance for it conveys a message from God, and a warning that acts as a guide. Before we explore the convergence of the stars in the Cosmic Crossroad, we will unravel a lesson on the Fig Tree which will point us to a 70-year prophetic period on the "Cosmic Cross-Road Chart," and the Prophetic Jubilee Timeline. The Cosmic Crossroad chart will link the Generational periods to the entire timeline of life. This timeline is both eternal and supernatural, and in turn goes through the center of each time-wheel discussed in Figure #6. God has clearly predetermined these dates and events to fulfill His promises and prophecy.

The 4 Arms of the Cosmic Crossroad Outline illustrates the crossroad of the entire timeline of life. This timeline is both eternal and supernatural, and in turn goes through the center of each time-wheel as will be shown in Figure 6. God predetermines each event to fulfill His promises and prophecy.

# The **COSMIC CROSSROAD**

| | The Fig Tree is the Nation of Israel | |
|---|---|---|
| Sun, Moon & Sign of Revelation 12 and Bethlehem Star | | Testimonies of Malachi, the Prophets, History, 10 Days of Awe, Jerusalem, Festivals and the Wilderness Tabernacle |
| | Biblical Generations & Jubilee Years | |

We seem to be at a very important "Cosmic Crossroad" in time, both astronomic and historical - linking God's time to man's time and joining Judaic prophetic signs to Gentile Signs of the End Time. Just as God used the stars to point us to His 1st Coming, does it not make sense that He will again use the stars and constellations to point to us **His 2nd Coming!**

**Figure #1** above shows a Crossroad linking the past, present, and future events to: God's Great Sign and Promise, the mysterious Fig Tree parables, and the many prophetic Testimonies. His chosen messengers which include His prophets and Apostles, and various Divine time markers. God has inspired and directed many of the great men and women of history to fulfill His Promises. And when He needs extra help, He uses the weather as in the case of D-Day, Valley Forge, and the Spanish Armada. Through His Word, He invites us to explore with Him the depth of His Power and Truth. He encourages us by declaring, *"All the treasures of wisdom and knowledge are found in Christ Jesus."* His Message, the holy Spirit that He left behind, and the wonder of His Creation can bring us great joy. By exploring this Message, we can experience His intimacy and Love for us. With this Love, we can grow in faith and help others.

Faith will allow us to walk through the *fire* of trials with Him. While writing this book I was overcome by fear when one late night as I was typing the number 666 came up in bright blue in the center of my page. After some panic, I was able to stop the *virus* and isolate it. The book was saved. Proverbs 3:5-6 says, *"Trust in the Lord with all your heart, lean not on your own understanding and He will make your path straight."*

He invites us to explore with Him the depth and width of his wisdom so that our path will be right on target! Just do not lean on what the world has taught you and what you think is true and the only answer. He alone is the Author of faith, truth, and prophecy. Prophecy gives us Hope for through it we can know God's Power over Time as He alone is the *Beginning and End, Omnipresent, and Omniscient.*

I want people to know how urgent this message is for there are sinister forces spreading throughout the world causing havoc. We have a choice to either let fear or anxiety control the future, or to seek out a personal relationship with God who has been trying to get our attention. He gave us ample warning in His Word and in the Great Sign in the stars. The Sign reflects the very fact that He is in control. It distinctly warns that invisible forces are here and are going to affect our lives and the course of nations. The next paragraph of verses start with the incredibly significant word, *"Then."* This implies that the war in which Satan, the dragon, is permanently cast out of heaven happens right after the Great Sign. He and all his rebellious angels are defeated and thrown out of heaven by Michael the Archangel and his angels. And it states that Satan is angry and ready to strike out.

More than likely his anger is directed at both Israel and America, and at both the Jews and Christians. Is this why we are seeing a surge of strange, irrational events like our election and the tragedies that led up to the burnings, along with the riots, shootings and violence that followed? Is this a cause of changes in leadership all over the world?

We will learn more about this dragon-serpent and his connection to God's promise at the beginning of time. You will see that he is the one who tried to use Herod to kill the young Jesus and is now pursuing the church. The church is Jesus Christ on earth. God used the sacrifice of animals as a foreshadowing of the ultimate sacrifice made by Jesus Christ for us at the cross. He is giving us another foreshadowing now.

God wants you to know that even though these dark forces are real, His power, His angels, and the Holy Spirit are stronger. And He will keep His promises. There is great hope for anyone who chooses God, knows His Word, and prepares for a divine purpose. God expects us to share the Truth (His Promises) with others so that they can also have hope. God says, *"to be alert and of sound mind so that we can pray."* God wants us to use those opportune times of duress, suffering, and testing to pray with others and for others. He wants us to share the His Word with His Love and laced with Hope. Years of study in the Word of God, on the Biblical generations, the heavenly lights, the Sign of Woman of Revelation 12, and current events and history, have inspired and compelled me to write this book with great effort and deliverance.

# CHAPTER TWO

# The Mystery of the Fig
# Tree Prophecy

Picture Jesus Christ and his disciples as they journeyed down the dusty road back to Jerusalem. Jesus was hungry and he knew that the leaders of Israel would soon reject him, when he saw a fig tree on the wayside that had leaves, but no fruit he said, *"May no fruit ever come from you again*!" Matthew, then states, *"And the fig tree withered at once."* When the disciples saw it, they marveled, saying, "How did the fig tree wither at once?" And Jesus answered them, *"Truly, I say to you, if you have faith and do not doubt, you will not only do what has been done to the fig tree, but even if you say to this mountain, 'Be taken up and thrown into the sea,' it will happen. And whatever you ask in prayer, you will receive, if you have faith."* Mat: 21:19-22. Just the day before, Jesus had cleansed the temple and driven out the money changers.

Did the disciples connect this surprise cursing to those recent events? They had experienced oppression under a mix of both Roman and strict Herodian rule, especially Matthew the tax collector. They knew about the Temple tax and the history of the failures of their own kings and nation. Did they think Jesus was just giving them a quick lesson on faith and the possibility of being able to throw a *mountain* into the *sea? Yes*, it seems clear, Jesus was stating how important faith is, and *Yes*, he was also emphasizing how Faithful God is. However, beneath the obvious there was a powerful message for the near future concerning the religious leaders and the survival of the nation of Israel. This puzzling statement would acknowledge the diaspora of the Jewish nation throughout the Gentile world in the coming decades.

Let us first note that the curse of the fig tree was not the first and only time that Jesus cursed something. Jesus who said, *"For God did not send his Son into the world to condemn the world, but in order that the world might be saved through him,"* did curse the cities of Chorazin, Bethsaida, and Capernaum for their unbelief. Earlier in the history of Israel, God laid down blessings and curses on the nation of Israel.

He said, *"When all these come upon you, the blessing and the curse, which I have set before you. Obey his voice in all that I command you today with all your heart and with all your soul, then the LORD your God will restore your fortunes and have mercy on you, and he will gather you again from all the peoples where the LORD your God has scattered you."* Deut. 11:19-22.

God promises a blessing to those who obey him. He promised to restore the fortunes of the Israelites and gather them from every nation in the world! He made the same promise to Jacob that he had made to Abraham, *"I am the Lord, the God of your father Abraham and the God of Isaac. I will give you and your descendants the land on which you are lying. Your descendants will be like the dust of the earth, and you will spread out to the west and to the east, to the north and to the south. All peoples on earth will be blessed through you and your offspring,"* Gen. 28:13-14. I believe a partial fulfillment of these blessings was in 1947-48, when God reversed the diaspora and restored Israel (the mountain of Zion), drawing His people out from all the nations of the world (the sea)? This move of Jews back to Israel is not over.

Many believe that the blessing is still real today as the nation of Israel draws more and more Jews to a prosperous and fruitful land.

We shall soon see how this *budding* of Israel relates to the lesson of the Fig tree. We must first address the elephant in parenthesis. When Jesus spoke of the *mountain* and the *sea,* was he using clever allegories? Was Jesus making an indirect forecast of what was about to happen to the mountain known as *Zion*, and the nation of Israel?

Not long after His crucifixion, in the years 67-135 AD, from the Nero persecution to the Hadrian dispersion of 135 AD, the Jewish nation as it existed was thrown off Mount Zion and cast into the *sea* of the world's Gentile population. The Jews were soon dispersed throughout the Empire and beyond. All the disciples would die as martyrs prior to the destruction of Jerusalem except for John the Apostle.

It seems that Jesus was showing empathy towards John as He knew John would eventually be the lone survivor of the group. Looking back John would remember this moment and would understand what Jesus meant about the "mountain" and the "sea." On the Island of Patmos where he wrote the Book of Revelation, John would be a distant witness to the destruction on the *Mountain of Zion* and the Holy city of Jerusalem in 70 AD. John in fact would use the same word, *sea* to denote the vast population of the earth as he wrote the prophetic book. And he would also use the word *mountain* to represent the ruling power. He would understand that the mountain that was cast into the sea were his people, the Jewish nation, which would be dispersed among the gentile nations of the world.

As John penned Revelation in exile on the volcanic Isle of Patmos, he would fully comprehend the meaning of the allegory "casting the Mountain" into the sea. John would use the same word "sea" to denote the vast population of the earth. He understood that the "Mount cast into the sea" was Mount Zion, his Jewish nation, which would be dispersed into the Gentile world. One irony is that his mountain Isle of Patmos was cast up from the Sea by the fire of volcanic action, whereas Israel would eventually be cast out of the fire of Trial and Suffering from this Sea of Nations.

Let us now do a quick study of some general applications in the Bible concerning the fig and the fig tree. Most people remember Adam and Eve used a fig leaf to cover up their nakedness. It is interesting that fig trees have both male and female fruit with the female fruit having an ovary and the male a stamina. The Fig tree is a very hardy tree that can handle dry climates and can produce three crops a year. The fig tree itself with its large leaves has a canopy effect that acts as a great shade tree. Figs and fig trees play a big part in life of people in that day. It is no surprise that God used both as symbols and signs.

In the book of Jeremiah, he warns about the good figs and the bad figs in Judah. The Lord told Jeremiah that the good figs are the Judah exiles who would be protected and brought back to Jerusalem. *"They shall be my people and I will be their God, for they shall return to me with their whole heart."* But the bad figs were those who ignored the prophets and stood by the *evil* king Zedekiah. They were to be *"made a horror to all the kingdoms of the earth—and I will utterly destroy them in the land that I gave to them and their fathers,"* Jer. 24:3-10. In the verse below God made a promise to Jeremiah, to keep his people in exile only 70 years. The people of Judah were not only granted passage back to Jerusalem, but they were also given protection, materials, their golden temple implements, and money with manpower to build the walls and restore the Temple. This is reminiscent of what Pharaoh ended up giving Israel, their slave nation, as God delivered them. Now in our time, thousands of years later, we are facing a similar return of Jews back to the homeland after another 70-year prophetic period and after the great Sign of Revelation 12. This migration or Aliyah has been predestined by God prior to His Return.

*"For thus saith the LORD, that after seventy years be accomplished at Babylon, I will visit you, and perform my good word toward you, in causing you to return to this place. For I know the thoughts that I think toward you, saith the LORD, thoughts of peace, and not of evil, to give you an expected end."* Jeremiah, 29:10, The good figs represent

people like the prophet Daniel, Shadrach, Meshach and Abednego and others like Ezra, and Nehemiah who led the restoration of the Temple and Jerusalem and eventually reestablished the nation of Israel. These "good figs" became the new Judah and eventually the nation of Israel. Throughout prophecy God did everything possible to draw the attention of His people, yet the majority ignored the warning signs and destruction came upon them over-and-over again. Do we want to ignore the warning signs that God is using to point out our rebellion and the sin in our lives? Will we miss the caution signs that He places to guide and direct us?

We are being struck by extreme weather, irrational behavior by once ethical institutions, the breakdown of the family, the lifting up of perversion and lies, the cancel culture to erase history, and the pushing down of truth and Christianity. These may be harbingers of approaching trials and testing. Jonathan Cahn, the author of The Harbinger, makes a strong case suggesting that the attack on 9/11 was a harbinger of things to come and that we have forsaken our Christian heritage and foundation. He discusses the Sycamore fig tree that saved St. Paul chapel from destruction. This is the same chapel where George Washington and the Congress prayed on a Geneva Bible for the new nation. *"Before God judges a nation, He sends a warning,"* Rabbi Cahn said. *"But America, like Israel, has not responded with repentance, but with defiance."* We are seeing this defiance being magnified tenfold in this present day and age! And it seems as if Christianity, prayer, and the Bible are big targets.

Now like a light shining onto distant skies, the Fig tree reappears in prophecy and focuses on the second coming of Jesus Christ. The prophecy in Zachariah 3:8-9, is directed to every Jew throughout the world like a signpost that gives the actual name of the Messiah! Zachariah the prophet addresses the leader and high priest of the final expedition to sanctify the Temple. As stated earlier, Jerusalem and the Temple were rebuilt with the help of the faithful who traveled from Persia with the golden temple implements, money, tools, and craftsmen. It is the first time and only time in history that a conquering Empire openly reached out with all its might to protect, supply, and repopulate a defeated nation's capital city and Temple for the benefit of those it had held in servitude.

Zachariah recognized that only God could have done this. He says to the people, *"Hear now, O Joshua the high priest, you and your friends who sit before you, for they are men who are a sign: behold, I will bring my servant the Branch... declares the LORD of hosts, and I will remove the iniquity of this land in a single day. In that day, declares the LORD of hosts, every one of you will invite his neighbor to come under his vine and under his fig tree."* Zech. 3:8-9

The *Branch* is a direct reference to Jesus Christ who is the shoot that sprouts out of the stump of Jesse, the father of David. Isaiah 11:1, states, *"There shall come forth a shoot from the stump of Jesse, and a branch from his roots shall bear fruit."* The fruit was born through the David's line leading to the *Son of David*, Jesus Christ. The "fruit" is the Church or the *Bride of Christ* which includes the *Seed* of Abraham. The High Priest Joshua would be the one to sanctify the newly restored Temple. This is a parallel picture of Jesus who restores and sanctifies our body, the temple of the Holy Spirit. It is interesting to note that Joshua has the same root meaning in Hebrew as the name Jeshua or Jesus. There is also an interesting parallel to the nation of Israel today and the miracle restoration of Judah as a nation. In Zechariah's time, they were reluctant to leave the comfort of Babylon, and likewise, today many Jews do not want to leave the comfort of America. Most have grown secular and distant from God. If only they would open their Old Testament, and read about Daniel, Isaiah, Zechariah, and the other messengers that God sent to teach us about His truth and love. He has sent us signs and storms to warn us of more testing, trials, and purging to come. What we think is global warming is really is really God trying to get our attention. He wants us to turn to him so that we will learn to trust in Him. And it is interesting how recent storms have veered towards Washington DC and New England. His prophecies are windows into the future.

*"Now in the first year of Cyrus king of Persia, that the word of the LORD by the mouth of Jeremiah might be fulfilled, the LORD stirred up the spirit of Cyrus king of Persia, so that he made a proclamation throughout all his kingdom and also put it in writing: 'Thus says Cyrus king of Persia, 'The LORD, the God of heaven, has given me all the kingdoms of the earth, and he has charged me to build him a house at Jerusalem, which is in Judah. Whoever is among you of all his people, may the LORD his God be with him. Let him go up."* 2 Ch 36:22-23. King Cyrus was appointed by God, for both his name and mission were in Isaiah's prophecy 250 years earlier. Isaiah called Cyrus, *God's Shepherd*, or the *Lord's Anointed* before he was even born. This is one of the amazing wheels of Prophecy that God uses to impact even nations. In this case, Cyrus was made king of the mighty Persian Empire at the time needed for the reconstruction of Jerusalem and its temple. Later, Alexander the Great at the point of launching an attack on Jerusalem was read the prophecy of Daniel by the Priests at the gate. On seeing that God had predetermined that he a Greek warrior would conquer Persia quickly and decisively, was encouraged to spare the city.

There is another important message in Zechariah's prophecy, and it shines a light further into the future. As stated, the high Priest Joshua sanctified the new Temple known as Zerubbabel's Temple. In Zechariah's passage God states that he will fulfill His promises and will restore the land in just one day on that great *Day of the Lord*. That day will mark the beginning of the Millennium. I find it significant that this promise and prophecy is connected to a remarkable under the fig tree allusion. Is God using this fig tree image to focus a light on *Grace and Rest* that Jesus Christ freely offers to all who believe? Jesus says, *"Behold I stand at the Door and knock. If anyone hears My voice and opens the door, I will come into him and dine with him, and he with me. To him who overcomes I will grant to 16 sit with Me on My throne..."* Rev. 3:20-21. Salvation is not just for a moment, it is for eternity and involves the blessing of Life in Him and with Him, even before heaven. He seeks us under the *fig tree of life* to comfort us and give us rest; and will dwell in us and dine with us.

It is important to understand the full meaning of the *Vine* and the *Fig Tree*. Since God is talking about the land in the Millennium it makes sense that He is talking about His promise to Israel in the Old Testament. In the Old Testament Israel was represented by the vine or the vineyard. A good example is the book of Isaiah: God states, *"For the 'Vineyard 'of the Lord of Hosts is the 'House of Israel, 'and the men of Judah (Jews) His 'Pleasant Plant'(Vine),"* Isa. 5:7. Here we see that the *House of Israel* is the Vineyard and the Vine is Judah.

However, we must note two other verses and two very important points: God warns the nation of Israel of His judgment: *"And now go to; I will tell you what I will do to my Vineyard: I will take away the hedge thereof, and it (the Vine) shall be eaten up; and break down the wall thereof, and it (the Vineyard) shall be trodden down; and I will lay it WASTE: it shall not be pruned, nor dug out; but there shall come up briers and thorns: I will also command the clouds that they rain no rain upon it,"* Isa. 5:5-6! God destroyed the *Vineyard*, which is Israel and laid it to waste. Even today the land lacks the beauty of its glory days when the trees sang in praise. God had always wanted His chosen people to be an example to the rest of the world, but they became a sore and a wasteland in the eyes of God, and so he gave them what they wanted. Why should God ever again use the symbol of the vineyard to represent His people?

Israel disobeyed God and went their own way. The nation was destroyed except for a righteous remnant which came from the tribe of Judah. This purging was done to purify Israel and the land. As earlier stated, God was keeping His promise to keep a remnant to carry forth the *Seed* and the blessing. He has fulfilled this promise throughout the ages. This brings us to the next important point that will again apply to the Fig Tree and to us today. We have already noted multiple examples of how the past repeats itself and comes around like a wheel into the present or the future!

After the return from the Babylonian exile Judah becomes Israel. As discussed, they are the righteous remnant that God uses to rebuild his nation. In the New Testament Jesus uses the vineyard to symbolize the Palestine wasteland, and the Fig Tree to represent the Jewish nation. Jesus told his disciples this parable: *"A man had a fig tree that had been planted in his vineyard. He went to look for fruit on it but did not find any. So, he told the gardener, 'Look here! For three years I have been coming to look for fruit on this tree but have not found any. Cut it down! Why should it waste the soil?' But the gardener replied, 'Sir, leave it alone for one more year, until I dig around it and fertilize it. 'Maybe next year it will bear fruit. If not, then cut it down.'"* Luke 13:6-9. The owner of the Vineyard or the Kingdom of God, and of the Fig-tree or the nation of Israel, is God. He came in the person of Jesus Christ, who is the Gardener. For three years of His ministry, Jesus had searched for fruit from the Jewish nation, but found none. Instead, they rejected Him. God therefore decided to cut down the tree, which is the unfruitful nation of Israel.

However, instead of putting the axe to tree, God gave the nation a 40-year reprieve of testing and purifying until the year AD 70, at which time the nation was thrown down and *"cast into the sea"* by the Roman general Titus. The axe was laid only at the root of the *Tree*, as stated by Luke. The root itself was not killed nor removed from the soil. The nation could grow back in 1948. The budding *Fig Tree* is the nation of Israel which will again face purification and purging.

The Jewish nation had become so indoctrinated to life under excessive man-made laws and works that they felt the compulsion to perform moment by moment. The Zechariah passage discussed earlier was a subtle message of Grace for them. Reread the verse again: *"Every one of you will invite his neighbor to come under his vine and under his fig tree."* The possessive *his* has a double meaning and may refer to Jesus Christ, as the Branch, and the owner of his or her vine or fig tree. *"Under His vine and Under His Fig Tree,"* points to the future when Jesus is Lord of both the vine and the fig tree, which from our New Testament perspective represents the Church (for we are grafted onto the vine) and the nation of Israel which is the fig tree.

This multiple meaning would be pointing to both Gentile and Jewish believer in the Millennium or in our present era of the Gospel of Grace. Could it simply refer to any wine and food dining experience during the Feast of Tabernacles? Or is it a reference to the Church and the redeemed Messianic Jews of today? Since the theme of this passage is the Millennium, it appears that this is a message of Hope and a New Beginning related to the 1000-year period when the Lord rules over a redeemed Kingdom on this earth. The New Beginning is one of the central themes of this book. God has a new Beginning promised to all who believe and trust in Him. He instituted a celebration of the Feasts to remind His people of this. Everything in the Holy Feast days point to the sacrificial death of Jesus Christ for He is the *First Fruit*, the *Bread of Life*, the *Fulfillment of the Law* on Mt. Sinai, the reconciliation of sinful man to God, the *Tabernacle*, who tabernacles within us, and the *New Beginning in His Grace*.

Ephesians 2:8-9 states, *"For it is by Grace through faith that we have been saved, it is NOT of works so that no one can boast."*

Does this prophetic light shine on the final fig tree parable stated by Jesus Christ in all 3 Synoptic Gospels? There are very few parables repeated in all three Gospels. It seems that God is using this simple fig tree prophecy to shine a powerful prophetic light onto a final fig tree promise. This lesson is relayed by Jesus in the Olivet Discourse which occurred on the Mount of Olives - the very same Mountain upon which Jesus will set foot when He returns as the Lion of Judah! This mountain faces Jerusalem and Mount Zion on the East and alongside it runs the road that continues to Bethany where Jesus often stayed with Mary, Martha, and Lazarus.

The cursed and withered fig tree may have been perched on the road traversing the Mount of Olives. With Jerusalem in sight Jesus will use this withered fig tree as part of a more powerful message linking both the fig tree lesson on faith to the next fig tree lesson on prophecy spoken on the Mount of Olives. After warning about birth pains, wars and rumors of wars, famines, false prophets, the Tribulation, the second coming of the Lord, and even the *"abomination of desolation,"* Jesus says, *"Now learn this lesson from the fig tree."* By now He has gotten the attention of the disciples and continues, *"As soon as its twigs get tender and its leaves come out, you know that summer is near. Even so, when you see all these things, you know that it is near, right at the door. Truly I tell you, this generation will certainly not pass away until all these things have happened,"* Mat 24: 32-34.

What could possibly be so important about a fig tree that Jesus feels the need to share it in the same breath as His extensive End Time prophecy? First, we must understand that the Fig tree prophetic lesson was not fulfilled in 70 AD., nor at any time since! We have not experienced a world-wide *Tribulation*, the *Abomination of Desolation*, the 2nd coming of Christ, nor the destruction of the Earth and the Millennium. Hence this Prophecy has not been fulfilled. I must state this emphatically, since some theologians and prophecy teachers claim that Jesus Christ has already returned in our hearts, therefore we are in the *spiritual millennium*. We all know that this mess of a world cannot be the Millennium.

We saw earlier that the first lesson on the Fig tree shared from Matthew 21, along with the prophecy in Zechariah 3, point to the Fig Tree as being the Nation of Israel. The *"cursed and withered fig tree,"* is Israel as it withered at the hands of Roman persecution from 70-85 AD. The *"budding fig tree"* in Matthew 24:32, is the Nation of Israel reborn or reestablished in 1947- 48! Hence the *"generation"* that *"will not pass until are these things are fulfilled"* is the post-World War II generation that rebuilt, America, Europe, Asia, Russia, Israel and basically the whole world. This is the generation that has fulfilled the Great Commission and spread the Gospel throughout the earth. We are in this prophetic generation and by God's grace have been given extra time as new souls are saved and the anti-Christ prepares his entrance.

Our generation is an 80-year generation called the Baby Boomers. This has been the Generation of New Beginnings starting with Israel and now most recent continuing with the Sign of Revelation 12 and the "invisible attack" that it portended. On the flip side this is also the generation that experienced or lived through the Holocaust and the constant threat of world-wide destruction.

If we consider 1947-48, as the rebirth or budding of Israel, and we add 70 prophetic years we come to 2017! This lesson spoken by Jesus in Matthew 24, Mark 13, and Luke 21, points to our present time. The Mystery of the Fig Tree is thus revealed. Soon we will see how God uses numbers like 70-weeks, or 70 sevens, to represent 490 years and how Daniel's last week or 7 years has not been fulfilled. These are prophetic periods that God has not yet fulfilled. He will keep his promises and we shall soon see why those last 7 years are so important! Like Daniel and the rest of the Judah remnant, we are aliens in a land that is only a temporary rest, until He guides us to New Beginnings. Next, I will show how there are other layers including the Biblical Generations, the Stars, the Rabbi, and other prophetic testimonies which point to an approaching End Time event. Reference the Cosmic Crossroad Chart in Figures 4 and 5.

We could be the generation witnessing the number of martyrs of Revelation 6:9, being fulfilled. The Lord reveals that His Wrath will wait until that number is reached. The Lord states, *"They were told to rest a little while longer until the number of their fellow servants and brothers, who were going to be killed just as they had been, would be completed."* It is tragic that so many Christians are being martyred amid this age of reason. The irrational behavior of people throughout the world seems to be increasing at an alarming rate. Is this a supernatural invasion by demon spirits?

In the next chapter, we are going to Look Up into the starry darkness to study the stars and Signs. We will see the dragon which represents Satan or the Serpent. This is a good time to forewarn you that like any Sign or parable there is a lot left to interpretation. Like a parable there is more to understanding the stars than just looking at a telescope or reading a book. Here is what the Old Testament prophet Isaiah and the Son of God had to say about parables. Jesus answered the disciples, "*To you it has been granted to know the mysteries of the kingdom of heaven, but to them it has not been granted. For whoever has, to him more shall be given, and he will have an abundance; but whoever does not have, even what he has shall be taken away from him. Therefore, I speak to them in parables; because while seeing they do not see, and while hearing they do not hear, nor do they understand.*" Jesus is quoting Isaiah when he says, "*Hearing you will hear and shall not understand, and seeing you will see and not perceive; For the hearts of this people have grown dull. Their ears are hard of hearing, and their eyes they have closed, lest they should see with their eyes and hear with their ears, lest they should understand with their hearts and turn, So that I should heal them. 'But blessed are your eyes, because they see; and your ears, because they hear. For truly I say to you that many prophets and righteous men desired to see what you see, and did not see it, and to hear what you hear, and did not hear it,*" Matthew 13:10-17. Committed prayer and a dedication to studying and applying His Word is a good start to understanding signs and parables. God will meet us at the heart.

God has helped us share the Gospel on a weekly basis at our neighborhood lake for the last 12 years. Our mission is called *Answers on the Rock*, and as we pray and teach, we give away free lemonade, and free inspirational books for adults and children. Conversations about salvation, hope, truth, forgiveness, and other matters of the heart have become a big catalyst to inspire thoughts that only God could have given us. Recently God inspired me to encourage a new believer who had questions on prophecy and its value to us today. As I shared from my heart the parable of the fig tree, I was struck by its import in a much deeper way than I had viewed it before. Yes, while I was speaking God was teaching my heart knowledge that I had not yet grasped in my mind!

Likewise, God moved my heart and mind to share what He revealed concerning the Sign of Revelation 12. The message was put in my heart by the Holy Spirit, and nothing can stop me from revealing this message to the church and to the world. We do not have much time as God prepares the earth for His Return and for the coming time of lawlessness.

# CHAPTER THREE

# Revelation 12: A Unique Converging of Sun, Moon & Stars

We seem to be at a particularly important *Cosmic Crossroad* in time, both astronomical and historical - linking God's time to man's time and joining Judaic prophetic signs to Gentile Signs of the End Time. Just as God used the stars to point us to His first coming, does it not make sense that He will again use the stars and constellations to point us to His Second Coming? The fact is all of us are looking for understanding and for a little piece of heaven in our hearts, but many of us do not quite realize that. I did not! At least not until I surrendered my life over to God, then hearing came by the Word of God and faith by hearing Christian radio and ministries. I know that even simple words can bring a little bit of heaven to us, so let us delve into this starry realm to see if there is indeed a little bit of heaven here, and hopefully some near you. Have you ever prayed, *"Thy kingdom come, thy will be done on Earth as it is in Heaven?"*

At the first coming, the Stars announced His birth, an event that changed the earth forever and introduced us to the Lamb of God who opened the Door to Heaven and introduced us to the Lamb of God who opened the Door to Heaven. The Stars were a Sign of the Son who was undiscovered until the Magi found him at the age of about 2. The people and leaders in the area did not notice these Signs, nor the spectacular birth. Therefore, it is entirely possible that the present Sign will not catch the attention of our leaders nor generate events that will be connected back to it. The journey by the Magi took months, yet the stars remained as a signpost. Will there be other signs *in the stars* soon? The star maps do show any evidence of this.

January 12, 2017, started off with a "Wolf Moon," the first full moon of the year. Also, the planet Venus was at its brightest in eight years. Both events occurred the evening before Friday 13th. This was bracketed by many surprises including the Trump victory and three worldly *Returns* or *Reversals of fortune*: The Miss Universe contest. the Oscars, and climatic fall of the Falcons during the Super Bowl! This is clearly a time of the unexpected and the return or surrender of laurels and expectations. God has warned us to put our treasures in heaven and not in this world. He wants us to Glorify Him and be ready. We will see how these signs and others point forward to 2024 and 2027.

All these signs have been placed on our *timeline* to catch our attention. I call this the wheel of *Signs in the Stars and Constellations*. My desire is NOT to scare you, but to inform you and lift your spirit and your interest in the supernatural so that you will focus on God's message to us. These converging celestial signs are just more evidence that the Jewish Jubilee and Shemitah are crossing over into the Gentile world. We are presently in the Prophetic 70-year period mentioned in Chapter 2, and the final Jubilee year of *Returns* which we will discuss in the next chapter. Yes, 2017 is the year that all land was to be returned to the original owner - the one God appointed to have the land, or as in the case of the *vineyard* mentioned earlier, returned to be purified by God himself. Is God ready to purify our generation or to purify the earth? It does seem that the sign is intended for both Israel and for the Gentile world.

*"They were unaware until the flood came and swept them all away, so will be the coming of the Son of Man. Then two men will be in the*

*field; one will be taken and one left. Two women will be grinding at the mill; one will be taken and one left."* Matt. 24:41

Revelation 12:1-4, states, *"A spectacular sign appeared in the sky: a woman dressed in the sun, who had the moon under her feet and a victor's crown of twelve stars on her head. She was pregnant and was crying out from her labor pains, the agony of giving birth. Then another sign appeared in the sky: a huge red dragon with seven heads, ten horns, and seven royal crowns on its heads. Its tail swept away one- third of the stars in the sky and knocked them down to the earth. Then the dragon stood in front of the woman who was about to give birth so that it could devour her child when it was born."*

In Genesis, 3:15, God says to the Serpent, *"And I will put enmity between you and the woman, and between your seed and her seed; He shall bruise you on the head, and you shall bruise him on the heel."* Obviously the "dragon" and "serpent" are the same and refer to Satan or the *Son of Perdition*. Will the sign of the Woman on September 23, 2017, fulfill this prophetic message?

The Sign of Revelation 12 in the Constellations Virgo and Leo has many details that are common, but unique when all are put together. The first part of the sign is the woman clothed with the sun. The sun is rising and appears as the new moon fades out along with the constellation. This happens every year, but it narrows the time down to one month around the autumnal equinox when the constellation is low on the horizon, allowing the sun to move into place. That woman is represented by Virgo. She is *clothed by the sun* from mid-September to early October. September 23, 2017, meets these requirements. Note the sun has to be low on the horizon in order for the other signs to show and even then, it will show for only minutes.

The next requirement is that the moon must be under the feet of Virgo. With the sun in Virgo and her feet to the east, the moon must be a couple of days past new moon since the Hebrew Calendar is lunar and the Feast of Trumpets, September 20-22, 2017, is on the new moon. September 23rd places the moon in the correct position.

This happens every year on the Hebrew Calendar if the new moon did not occur too early or too late in relation to the equinox, which would put the sun too high or low in Virgo. Here it is perfect. The requirement of the moon and sun narrows it down to a few days of the year. On September 23, 2017, there are four planets in the vicinity that complete the sign and its ultimate uniqueness: Mercury, Venus, Mars, and Jupiter. September 23rd is the first full day that all the Signs are in place. It so happens that this day is also the first complete day after the Jewish New Year begins and the Holy Jubilee of the 50-year period 1967-2017, ends. *"I, Jesus, have sent my angel to give this testimony for the churches. I am the Root and the Offspring of David, and the bright Morning Star (Venus),"* Revelation 22:16.

Graph Figure 2 on the next page illustrates the position of the 12 wandering lights at Virgo's head, the Sun at her shoulder, the new moon at her feet, the special Stars (Spica and Regulus), Jupiter, and the comet 67-P which is like a check mark in the sky. Jupiter plays a unique role in remaining in the womb of Virgo for over 9 months then exits on September 9th. For 400 days it traveled across the heavens with Venus in a conjunction. They entered Virgo together signifying Jesus as both High Priest and King of Kings.

This illustration shows Jupiter already outside the womb of Virgo. All is set for the sun to move into place. Did you know that the ancient Egyptians built the Sphinx as a window into the heavens? The Sphinx has the head of the virgin and the body of a lion. Virgo and Leo were believed to tie the heavens together. In between the two constellations of stars was the entrance to the afterlife where every Pharaoh sought special entry for himself and his family.

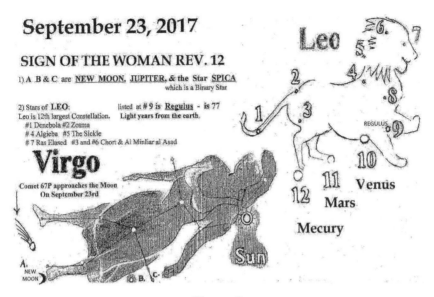

## September 23, 2017

### SIGN OF THE WOMAN REV. 12

1) A ,B & C are NEW MOON, JUPITER, & the Star SPICA
which is a Binary Star

2) Stars of LEO:                listed at # 9 is Regulus - is 77
Leo is 12th largest Constellation.   Light years from the earth.
#1 Denebola #2 Zosma
# 4 Algieba  #5 The Sickle
# 7 Ras Elased  #3 and #6 Chort & Al Minliar al Asad

## Virgo

Comet 67P approaches the Moon
On September 23rd

Leo

REGULUS

Venus

Mars

Mecury

NEW MOON

Sun

**Figure 2**

The Great Sign of the Woman of Revelation 12 is the most significant sign given to mankind by God. It links Genesis to Revelation- the Beginning to the End- and for that reason God placed it right in the middle of Revelation to John the Apostle. John was only a teenager when he began his journey with Jesus Christ and was an old man when he ended this journey after witnessing a vision of the Lord's Second Coming, the Millennium, and the end of the Earth.

He saw the image of the Woman and child and then immediately afterwards he saw Satan being cast from heaven. Will the Sign reflect this as the supernatural lawlessness that Jesus warned about when he spoke to John on the Mount of Olives? If this is the case, then the Sign of Revelation 12 is *Not In Chronological Order* with events in the Trumpet and Seal Judgments. Otherwise, how could Satan be leading his evil retaliation on earth during events in chapter 6 and the trumpets in chapter 9? Satan had to have been kicked out of heaven and released on earth before the Wrath begins. It is implied that he is helping the instigate lawlessness, helping the anti-Christ spirit on the white horse, and the terrorist-like character on the red one. As Peter states, *"Satan is like a roaring lion,"* and Jesus warned that Satan has come to *"kill, steal and destroy."* Satan is the lawless one creating lawlessness.

The astronomical scenario is extremely rare! What I am about to show you in the coming chapters will be even more convincing, especially when we understand the importance of the fig tree lesson already discussed. Could this coming star array be the same as when Adam and Eve walked with God in the Garden of Eden, as God spoke to them, revealing His Plan and naming each star and their meaning?

Jupiter is the key to this rare time-keeper sign from God. As the largest of all planets, it was known by the Jews as the planet *of Divine Authority*. To us it would represent the title of King of Kings. Venus of course is the *Bright Morning Star* ascribed to the Eternal Priest, Jesus Christ. Jupiter enters the sign of Virgo on August 27, 2016, along with a close conjunction of Venus, making this a much brighter and glorious entry. The conjunction of these two unique planets starts 400 days before Yom Kippur, September 30-31, 2017. Yom Kippur always ends Teshuvah, which is a 40-day season of repentance beginning on Aug. 21, 2017. Some observers like to combine these two prophetic numbers: dividing the prophetic 400-day length by the 40-day length of repentance to say that there is a ten-fold need of required repentance necessary at this period of time?

Note that repentance will always bring new beginnings with God and that is what all the signs point to. Remember also that the Jubilee year ends the day before the Sign appears. So, there is also a focus *"Returns."* Maybe something surprising is returned from one party to another such as land or the city of Jerusalem.

Can all these Signs be pointing to a Divine Appointment soon to occur? I think so, especially when you consider the blood moons and convergence of events. *"He counts the number of the stars; He gives names to all of them,"* (Psalm 147:4). What does all of this portend for Israel? What force will threaten them? The next such conjunction with these two bright planets will happen 49 years from now. Jupiter itself enters Virgo about every 12 years thus making it another 12-point wheel of time. When it enters Virgo, it is usually for a much shorter length of time and without the extensive retrograde movements, the *labor pains* as written in Revelation 12: 2.

Jupiter, acting as the largest planet and the one with Divine Authority, spends just over 9 months in the womb of Virgo, 294 days to be exact. The *"child"* of Rev. 12 will be *"born"* below it with the constellation Drago, the Serpent Dragon, waiting to devour it! By September 23, the *labor pains*, represented by the extensive retrograde movements of Jupiter have ended and the moon is in place. These retrograde patterns are caused by our earth moving faster around the sun than Jupiter. Jupiter, representing the child, exits Virgo on September 9. What does this portend? The *child* is vulnerable, and so this suggests that the church is ripe for a pursuit by the *dragon*. The child here is not the baby Jesus.

Could the recent blood moons that appeared in America, Asia, Europe, and the Middle East be a proclamation to the Jews who have forsaken God and not returned to their *Promised Land* to now *"gather from the 4 corners of the earth,"* and return to Zion? Likewise, could these Blood moons be a foreshadowing or a caution sign to the church and the whole world of an approaching message from heaven such as the four winds? Zechariah 6 speaks of winds and warns of four chariots, two going North, one South, and one remains nearby. Is America or Europe the destination of one or two of the chariots assigned to go North?

Venus separated earlier from Jupiter and moves out of Virgo. It moves into position with Mars and Mercury as shown on the illustration, Figure 2. On August 21, 2017, the United States has a Solar eclipse that travels like a divine slash from the upper west to the lower East coast, which one must admit is just about the longest possible exposure to American soil possible by a solar eclipse. It is in fact the first solar eclipse to cross from coast to coast in the U.S. for almost 100 years! God has purposed that this great American Solar

Eclipse happens the same day as the beginning of Teshuva, a Jewish time for repentance, linking the Gentile and Jewish paradigms. Teshuva is a time of personal reflection of one's sins. Is this a warning to a secularized America, to the compromised Jew, the weak church, and an overconfident community of godless, technology dependent agnostics? If no repentance, will this initiate massive storms and other disasters in America?

A triple emphasis including: the Venus and Jupiter conjunction, the solar eclipse, and the 40-day Jewish time of repentance, are all related to the date Aug. 21, 2017! Are they interrelated? Could the number 21 be significant, since it keeps showing up: 7 + 7 + 7 = 21 or 3 units of 7? Sevens also play a big role in prophecy especially in the book of Revelation where it is used over 50 times! Another connection to 21 is that the 21st brightest Star in our sky is the star named "Regulus" which is the star at the virtual heart of the Constellation Leo. It is one of the 12 stars adorning the head of Virgo during the Sept. 23rd sign. The meaning of this star, which is at the center of earth's spin is the Kingly Star. Like the star Spica, God preserved its original name for us.

A powerful set of signs was the 4 blood moons in 2014 and 2015! They began 3 ½ years prior to the God's Great Sign. The idea of a blood moon serving as an omen of the approaching end times comes partly from the Book of Joel, where it is written *"The sun will turn into darkness, and the moon into blood, before the great and terrible day of the Lord comes,"* Joel 2:31. Could God be trying to get the attention of both Gentile and Jew through these and other approaching stellar events? These signs point to America but also to Israel and Jerusalem. An economic collapse, war, or other destabilizing event here or in the middle East will affect the church worldwide. *"And God said, let there be lights in the firmament of the heaven to divide the day from the night; and let them be for signs, and for seasons, and for days, and years,"* (Genesis 1:14).

The Blood moons of 2014-15 were called the *Lord's Perfect Sign* because there was perfect symmetry in their order of time each falling on one of God's Jewish Feast Days: from Passover of 2014 and 15 to the Feast of Tabernacles in 2014 and 2015! That last Blood Moon in 2015, was a super-moon, and it happened over the city of Jerusalem. Psalm 89 calls the moon *"God's Faithful Witness."* Zachariah and other prophets point to this Holy City, as where the Lord, *Faithful and True*, will set His feet on the Mount of Olives. The three earlier blood moons drew attention to the gentile world. Jerusalem is the oldest large city in the world next to Damascus which in prophecy will be laid to waste in a war prior to the Lord's Return. I believe that God has allowed the Dome of the Rock to be where it is, to preserve the city as it is, until He is ready for the last Temple to be built. This could happen if nations again attack Israel, or if there is an earthquake that damages the integrity of the Dome. If it is war, then it would probably lead to the Biblical destruction of Damascus as stated in Isaiah 17:1.

We are already seeing great distress in the region and on the Temple Mount where higher security has been implemented with metal scanners. The Islamists will not let Christians nor Jews pray on the Temple mount. There is also distress between the superpowers, between Arab states and their proxies, and between rebel groups. Then there are Hezbollah, Hamas, and other radical groups threatening the life and survival of people everywhere.

As stated earlier the star Regulus sits at the *heart* of Leo and it is both a double star and the 21st brightest star. Regulus is also the brightest star to be near the perfect ecliptic plane in relationship to the Sun. Jesus is both the Son of God and the Son of Man, and He is the King of Kings with *"eyes of fire."* He is the Light at the center of the Universe. Leo with its bright stars has its feet near the head of Drago, the Dragon. The Message coming from this array is: The Lion of Judah will rule and reign supreme throughout the Universe and will soon crush the head of the Serpent-dragon. Rev 2:18. *"These things saith the Son of God, who hath his eyes like unto a flame of fire."* There is an unusual LINE of Planets, Mercury for Messenger, Mars for Man, and Venus for the Eternal Sacrifice by the Highest of High

Priests, Jesus Christ, all pointing like an arrow to the royal heart of Leo the Lion and the star Regulus. This is an incredibly special alignment, and a possible, surprise meaning to the *Sign of Revelation 12*, will be revealed later in the book.

Reference back to Fig. 2, the star Regulus and the *heavenly lights* of Venus, Mars, Mercury are in alignment. When we study them and the Sun, Moon, and Stars we realize that we are a very *Privileged Planet*. Everything is perfectly placed to allow for life to flourish on this planet. Some of these purposed miracles include as follows: the moon-to-sun size and distance is perfectly matched to allow for stable rotation and solar eclipses; a perfect leaning spin provides protection and the right combination of day and night; a perfect distance from the center of the milky way protects us from lethal radiation and comet collisions; and our perfectly located magnetic poles protect us from destructive gamma rays. We also have the perfect sun which is not too hot nor to too big and is relatively stable.

We are also in the perfect location to observe and measure the Universe. Finally, we cannot leave out the simple fact that we are the only observable body in the universe with water. We have over 325 million, trillion gallons covering 75% of the earth. I ask any Big Bang theorist to explain how a ball of fire becomes a ball of water. At this time, I want to prepare the evolutionist and Old Earth enthusiast that I am not looking for a war of words, but only your attention, because a good young-earth scientist can produce as much evidence that disputes millions of years as you can to support your position. So just relax and allow your mind some imagination and a spirit of inquisitiveness.

*"He made the earth by his power. He established the world by his wisdom, and by his understanding he spread out the heavens,"* Jeremiah: 51:15.

On September 23rd, the Comet 67P approached the moon. This is the same comet that Europe failed to land its Rosetta probe on! Did God shake it off? God is not going to let Gentile powers control Jerusalem and His Promised Land. Note the number 67 and its relation to the 1967 liberation of Jerusalem. Jerusalem celebrates the 50th *"Jerusalem Day"* on May 24, 2017- as it will be one Jubilee since being liberated on June 7, 1967! Also note what happened on the Tisha B' Av of July 16, 1994: The Shoemaker Levi Comet broke into 21 pieces, bombarding Jupiter for 7 days, each impact stronger than a nuclear bomb. As before the number 21 is 7+7+7 or 777. In the next chapter, we shall see how important the number 7 is in God's timetable and plan. We will see that $7 + 7 + 7 + 7 + 7 + 7 + 7 = 49$ is the formula for the 7 Sabbath years leading to the 50th Jubilee year.

When those comets hit Jupiter secret talks were going on in Oslo, Norway to exchange Israel's land for peace (Oslo Accords). The peace accord in Oslo led to partial withdrawal from Gaza and possibly the assassination of Rabin in 1995. Ten years later the withdrawal from Gaza was completed by Minister Sharon who later the next year had a debilitating stroke. Some say these tragedies are connected to the strikes on Jupiter. Others connect hurricanes and other disasters in America to our government's initiative in Israel's *land for peace* deals. We cannot be sure of this, but it is interesting how many signs in the sky seem to affect Israel and anyone trying to take the Promised land away from them. Note that Tisha B 'Av and has been a sad day to the Jew throughout history because this is the day that the first and second Temples were destroyed, and the day that Jews were expelled first from England and then 200 years later from Spain.

*"Lift up your eyes on high and see: who created these? He who brings out their host by number, calling them all by name, by the greatness of his might, and because he is strong in power not one is missing."* (Isaiah 40:26)

The next diagram is a Clock or *Wheel of Time* showing that we do not have much time left. Note that if this were a calendar it would go counterclockwise. This clock starts at the beginning of the *Tetrad of Blood Moons* or 1st of four Blood Moons on April 15, 2014. The clock outlines a 3 ½ year foreshadowing which ends at *Rosh Hashana* 5777 and may forewarn us of another 3 ½ year period to follow. This second 3 ½ year shadow begins at *Sign of the Woman* on Sept. 23, 2017, and would continue beyond the year 5778 to the year 5780 or 2020-21 which is this coming election year cycle. The other 3 Blood Moons went to different parts of the world to act as a wake-up call for everyone on earth. Each of them falls on one of God's important festival dates related to God's Redemption of mankind.

The great American Solar Eclipse on Aug. 21, 2017 (just one month earlier) cast a narrow but very wide physical shadow across the middle of America. Is this God's way to announce to the world that America will be the next step in His prophetic plan. Does it announce a *shadow* related to Daniel's final 7-year prophecy of two 3 ½ year periods? Are we in this prophetic foreshadowing?

Just as God's Creation on earth and in the stars glorify God, history and prophecy gives Him greater glory as events are fulfilled according to His Plan. He planned for His Great Signs to fall on Feast Days that would connect to both the Sign of the Woman and to the Jubilee years of Return. Prior to this were 2 Jubilee Years of Return which returned the land and the city of Jerusalem to its rightful owner, God's chosen people, the Jewish nation of Israel. This reminds us that God keeps His promises and is a motivation for Jews to return to Israel and for all who are lost to Return to Him. We will see more connections like this as we study the Generations, the Testimonies of God's Word, men and places, and the Fig Tree which is connected to the 70-year timeline. Each generational period including the 40, 50, 70, 80, 100, and 400 play a part in God's redemption.

In Figures 3A & 3B, *The Convergence of the Sun, Moon, and Stars with the Jewish Feast Dates and Festivals*, you will also notice a dotted line that begins on August 27, 2016, the date at which observers believe ISIS blew up the Palmyra gate and Temple area. This temple sacrifice compound was an important area of Baal worship and child sacrifice. This is the same area that Iran and Syria have a large air base with a drone fleet that Israel has repeatedly attacked.

This dotted line also marks the time that Jupiter (a sign of God's Authority) and Venus (the Priesthood of Jesus Christ - for He is the Eternal Priest and Sacrifice for us) join in a conjunction. This conjunction of heavenly bodies happened exactly 400 days prior to the Day of Atonement in August of 2017! As they rose together from the horizon in 2017 it stunned both the amateur and professional astronomers. Note that it also began 360 days prior to the Great American Solar Eclipse!

As stated earlier the first lunar eclipse in the 2014-2015 Tetrad was on Passover April 15, 2014. If you add 1260 days or 3 ½ years it falls on Sept 23, 2017! Not shown on the chart is the next 3-and-one-half year-period which goes beyond the inauguration and right up to the Spring Equinox on March 23, 2021. Will these next 3½ years warn of extensive New Beginnings? The blood moon occurred right next to the star Spica, meaning SEED, in Virgo, thus connecting God's prophetic sign in Gen. 3:15 to the Sign of the Woman. It all connects Passover, Israel, America, and God's redemption to these two Signs and to Jesus Christ, the Lion and Lamb of God.

Something else amazing is that this conjunction happens right next to the star formation called the *"Beehive."* In ancient days these stars, 83 which are bright, were called *"Praesepe"* which means multitude or offspring and includes the star that means hidden ones (like those who are protected by God prior to the Psalm 83 war.) Therefore, some believe that the overall meaning or picture of this cluster of stars which numbers in the millions may refer to those who are raptured. *The heavens declare the Glory of God; And the firmament shows His handiwork, Day unto day utters speech, and night unto night reveals knowledge, Psalm 19:1-2.*

On the next page is the **Figure 3A and 3B** which explains the unique convergence of Sun, Moon, Planets and Jewish Feast days.

# CONVERGENCE OF SUN, MOON & STARS WITH THE JEWISH FEASTS AND DATES

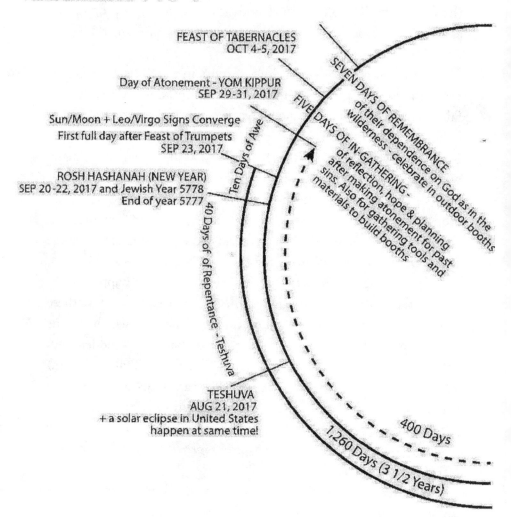

Many go to Jerusalem to celebrate

FEAST OF TABERNACLES
OCT 4-5, 2017

Day of Atonement - YOM KIPPUR
SEP 29-31, 2017

Sun/Moon + Leo/Virgo Signs Converge
First full day after Feast of Trumpets
SEP 23, 2017

ROSH HASHANAH (NEW YEAR)
SEP 20-22, 2017 and Jewish Year 5778
End of year 5777

Ten Days of Awe

40 Days of of Repentance -Teshuva

TESHUVA
AUG 21, 2017
+ a solar eclipse in United States
happen at same time!

SEVEN DAYS OF REMEMBRANCE of their dependence on God as in the wilderness- celebrate in outdoor booths

FIVE DAYS OF IN-GATHERING - of reflection, hope & planning after making atonement for past sins. Also for gathering tools and materials to build booths

1,260 Days (3 1/2 Years)

400 Days

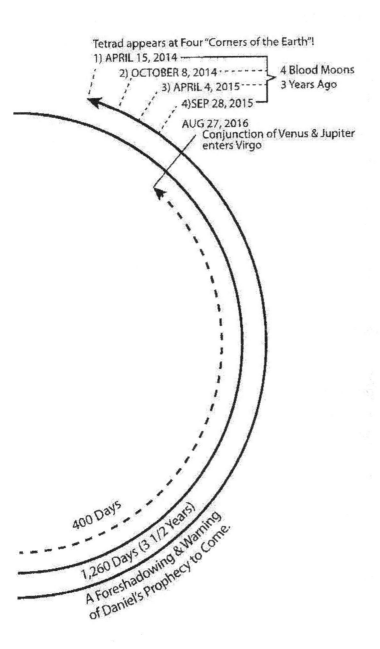

Tetrad appears at Four "Corners of the Earth"!
1) APRIL 15, 2014
2) OCTOBER 8, 2014
3) APRIL 4, 2015
4) SEP 28, 2015

4 Blood Moons
3 Years Ago

AUG 27, 2016
Conjunction of Venus & Jupiter
enters Virgo

400 Days

1,260 Days (3 1/2 Years)

A Foreshadowing & Warning
of Daniel's Prophecy to Come.

Jesus was sacrificed for us on Passover. He was the *Seed of the Woman* from Genesis 3:15, and since we are in Him, the church is also the seed of the woman. Both play a part in crushing Satan. Jesus was the ear of grain that must die that life may abound, and in a spiritual sense so are we. There is a spiritual connection between the harvest and the Jewish Feast Days, the blood moons, and other objects in space, as each plays a part in revealing the meaning of the Sign of the Woman. All of this is connected to both the "*Seed*" and "*Child*" and therefore to us. And it is the Lion or Leo that defeats the Dragon, Satan.

Theologians agree that "*The Woman*," Mary gave birth to a Son, Jesus Christ who defeated sin and is to rule with a rod of iron at least 2000 years after His birth. However, the next phrase *her child was caught up* or *rapturo* does not refer to the Ascension of Jesus Christas many scholars contend. Jesus had just defeated death and Satan and was NOT under any threat by Satan who is this *Dragon*. Jesus Christ, who is now in His Glorified body did not need to be *caught up*. This is important for you to understand - for this Promise transcends time as it points forward to a future rapture of the Church which will be *caught up* before the Dragon can destroy it. And this may be why God must speak His Voice today to people like you and me, because these self- proclaimed experts are not seeing nor proclaiming the Truth behind t the Signs that He wants His Church to see in order to warn the world.

Just like in Daniel's 70-week prophecy this puzzling End-Time prophecy unhitches from the first part of the verse and points to the future. This is not unusual for Jesus did that thing when he quoted Isaiah: "*The Spirit of the Lord is upon me...*" - which stops mid-verse with the last part of the promise to be fulfilled 2000 years later. Likewise, the child in the second part of the verse is now the *Church* which will be pursued and persecuted by Satan for hundreds of years. Hence the Great Sign is anchored in the past like a sign anchored in concrete. But it points to the future and NOT to the past as a sign should.

Jesus was *bruised*, but this was not a *defeat* for He conquered Death and Redeemed us from sin by His blood. A seed dies to bring new life. The star Spica (seed) in Virgo, reminds us of the reference to the *seed of the woman* in Genesis 3:15, and the *child* in Revelation 12:4. Both can have a double meaning but when putting everything in context, they refer to the church and not to Jesus himself. The seed of Abraham is the church. The *Serpent Dragon* represented by the Constellation Drago lies near the polar cap above Leo and Virgo and awaits the birth of the child. The passage indicates that the Dragon seeks to devour the child. The Dragon wants to persecute and destroy the church. Jesus was never in danger of being devoured by the Dragon, and as a baby Jesus was never *caught up* to heaven. The church is being pursued by Satan and to some extent is being devoured by him. However, the church will eventually be caught up will reign alongside Jesus Christ with His *rod of iron*.

The 12 stars are 12 tribes of Israel, the woman is Israel, and the sun according to some is Jacob, and the moon is Rachel who reflects the vision that Joseph had of the eleven stars. We saw earlier that the approaching feast days and their connection to the blood moons point to the September 23rd sign of Revelation 12. By studying the graph *"Convergence of Sun, Moon, and Stars with the Jewish Feasts and Dates,"* you will understand how all these events are connected.

The Sign of Revelation 12 is definitely a warning to us that an invisible attack is coming. If you believe in the Pre-Tribulation rapture, our time on earth could be cut short by the rapture to meet the Lord in the clouds. We have seen this in the wording of Rev. 12:1-3. As stated earlier the *woman* is collective Israel. The *Dragon* or Serpent is Satan and his armies of angels who battle Michael the Archangel in the book of Daniel and are shown again in battle against God in Revelation 12. The church needs defending because Satan wants to completely devour it. While studying Jupiter's position among the stars, there was something else that was evident and significant. Add seven prophetic years to the Jewish calendar from the 23rd day in September 2017, and you will have the 9th of Av, 2024. Jupiter will be in the sign of Taurus and it will not be in the sign of Virgo as it is now. It will sit between the horns along with Mars which is the symbol for Adam or the Son of Man. *"But you brothers, are not in darkness that this day should overtake you like a thief."* 1 Thessalonians 5:4

The common Hebrew name for Taurus the bull is "Shure," which can mean both the coming and the ruling or in other words, *The Coming Judge.* In short, Taurus could represent the Return of Jesus Christ as Judge, along with His congregation, represented by the adjoining Pleiades Star Cluster. The King comes with His church to Judge the World. This future sign could point to a time when Jesus will return to defeat the forces of the Anti-Christ. No other Celestial signs come into view after this time. All of this points to a sign suggesting the Lord's return could come in the twenties. Otherwise, there are few if any signs to match anything like this soon. *"It is like a man away on a journey, who upon leaving his house and putting his slaves in charge, assigning to each one his task, also commanded the doorkeeper to stay on the alert. Therefore, be on the alert—for you do not know when the master of the house is coming."* Mark, 13:34-35

We do know that God is in the business of purifying and redeeming mankind. We will soon see that Daniel's 70 weeks Prophecy was partially for purifying the prophetic generation during Daniel's time, but it was also for a future prophetic generation. This future generation is the *fig tree generation* of today. Since Daniel's generation was a prophetic 70-year generation, it would make sense that this special future generation or the *last generation* would also be a 70-year generation. I am not making predictions, but again I encourage everyone to dig into God's Word and Share the Gospel. Read the Book of Daniel to see how accurately God predicts history in Chapter 11 of his book. On the following page is Daniel's miraculous 70 Week Prophecy from God.

The Angel Gabriel gives Daniel the Prophecy of 70 weeks. The word in Hebrew for weeks is Sevens - so it is incorrect to say that it was 70-weeks since it could also mean 70-*Sevens* or 490 years-which is what most believe it means: "*Seventy weeks are determined upon thy people and upon thy holy city, to finish the transgression, and to make an end of sins, and to make reconciliation for iniquity, and to bring in everlasting righteousness, and to seal up the vision and prophecy, and to anoint the most Holy. Know therefore and understand, that from the going forth of the commandment to restore and to build Jerusalem unto the Messiah the Prince shall be seven weeks, and threescore and two weeks: the street shall be built again, and the wall, even in troublous times. And after threescore and two weeks shall Messiah be cut off, but not for himself: and the people of the prince that shall come shall destroy the city and the sanctuary; and the end thereof shall be with a flood, and unto the end of the war desolations are determined. And he shall confirm the covenant with many for one week: and in the midst of the week he shall cause the sacrifice and the oblation to cease, and for the overspreading of abominations he shall make it desolate...*" Dan. (9:24-27).

It is important to understand what this prophecy says. The reign of Artaxerxes began in 465 BC in the month of Nissan. Add twenty years and we have 445 BC. The command to rebuild Jerusalem was issued by Artaxerxes in 445 BC. Now we must add 7 weeks for the rebuilding of the walls which is 49 years or 7 X 7 =49. That now makes the date 396 BC. By the year 396 BC, God finally finished establishing the Temple, the Wall and city of Jerusalem, the Word, and His people. More information concerning this is found in the Old Testament books of Nehemiah and Ezra. Next, we need to consider the words "*Three score and two weeks,*" which is equal to 62 weeks. Add the 7 weeks and we have 69 weeks or 483 years. Now we must remember that the Jewish year was a 360-day- year, so we need to convert 483 years to days (360 X 483 = 173,880 days). Now to convert to a 365-day-year we divide 173880 by 365, and we get 476.4 years. Finally add 476 years and 3 months to 445 BC the date of Artaxerxes 'announcement. It points to the moment to the time Jesus Christ made his Triumphal entrance into Jerusalem in March of that year.

God gave Daniel the very day that the Messiah would make His Triumphal entry into Jerusalem. God's Calendar and Prophecy are exact, and it has yet to be completed. The 70th week or a 7-year period of two 3 ½ year- periods still awaits us. This will be a time of judgment lasting 7 years. The first period consists mainly of the Seal Judgments and the next 3½ year period is a combination of the *Day of the Lord* and the *Wrath of God*. We are presently in a 7-year Shemitah period after the first Jubilee of the 21st Century, which will end in 2024-25. This cold point to a Return to Daniel's prophecy of the 70th week, or to a foreshadowing of the return of the LORD. We will investigate this possibility and Daniel's prophecies more later.

*"Don't let anyone deceive you in any way, for that day will not come until the rebellion occurs and the man of lawlessness is revealed, the man doomed to destruction. He will oppose and will exalt himself over everything that is called God or is worshiped, so that he sets himself up in God's temple, proclaiming himself to be God,"* II Thessalonians 2:3-4. This implies that the first 3 ½ years follows a rebellion and a moment when the Anti-Christ exalts himself. However, he will not desecrate the Temple like Antiochus Epiphanes did in 167 BC. This new desecration will not be a pig but will be in the form of an image of the Anti-Christ. The important thing to note is the *lawlessness* mentioned.

Both Jesus in the Olivett discourse and Paul in his letter warns of lawlessness. We are seeing the roots of a future widespread lawlessness spread throughout America. This intensity is rising between liberals and right-leaning groups throughout the world. Here in America with so much media frenzy against one political party, we are preparing the fire for a major internal conflict. And there is deep division occurring all over Europe, Africa, South America Asia and even in Israel. It is a great spiritual turmoil or shaking of the *"sea."* In summary, we seem to be at an important Cosmic Crossroad in time, both astronomical- and historical - linking God's time to man's time and joining Judaic prophetic signs to *Signs of the Time* throughout the world.

Just as God used the stars to point to His 1st coming, does it not make sense that He will again use the stars and constellations to point to His 2nd Coming. He created the Universe with such precision and balance to make the earth a Perfect Planet for life. Our world is 24,000 (12,000 X 2) miles around and travels one million six hundred thousand miles in one day around the sun or 12 X 13,333 miles a day. Our moon which is key to tidal movements, currents, and weather changes on earth, has a linear diameter of 1,260 miles or 12 X 105 miles.

Twelve is the number of Perfection and Authority - but also of TIME set by God in the natural world of the moon, sun, stars, and constellations, (12 months, 12 Constellation Signs, and two sets of 12 hours). Twelve is an interesting number combination of the perfect unit of two found in all of creation and the number 10 of purification which we discussed concerning the 10 Days of Awe. Two is both a unit as in male and female, or the Hypostatic union of God and man, but it is also a divine contrast or balance between light and darkness, and good and evil. Thus, the number 12 could be defined as a number for order or balance in God's divine creation in both space and time.

By studying Science in the Light of His Word we can see the natural and the supernatural converging on these significant number Signs. Rev. 12 takes us back in time to His original warning in Gen. 3:15. God spoke to the Serpent and told him that his head would be crushed by the *Seed of the Woman*. This has not happened and when it does, it will eventually bring all creation back to perfection under the authority of the *Seed of Adam* who is Jesus Christ. The *seed of The Woman* is thus Israel who bore the Messiah, or the Seed of Adam. Since we are in Jesus and He is in us, the Seed in this sense is both Jesus and Church.

We will return with Jesus to crush Satan's minions. Jesus will crush his head. The Promises made by God in Genesis 3:15 and Revelation 12 seem to point to a moment in time reflected in both the stars and in our divinely set Solar Clock. As you continue to read you will see that all these numbers and number combinations connect us to a *Wheel in Time* that will bring all his Prophecy and Promises together on a divine timeline in history. Do you remember the Lord's prayer? Again, take note of the phrase, On *Earth as it is in Heaven* and keep that near your heart and mind. Our God is a God of order and Perfection which is reflected on this earth.

Since we will be discussing numbers and number sequences, it would seem appropriate to show you how ordered our surroundings are. The Fibonacci sequence is a great example of how God has orchestrated a perfect set of numbers to establish harmony in physics, biology, astronomy and just about every aspect of creation from the smallest leaf to the wide expanse of spiral galaxies. The Fibonacci sequence comes simply by adding the first or previous number to the next. $1 + 0 = 1$ and $1 + 1 = 2$, $2 + 1 = 3$, $3 + 2 = 5$ and so on. The sequence looks like this: 1, 1, 2, 3, 5, 8, 13, 21, 34 etc. God uses this ratio to define the shape and natural order of a wave as it breaks, curls in the shell of crustaceans, or the veins in leaf. We have a God who is in control and who holds all things together. *"He is before all things, and in him all things hold together."* This is one good reason why we have science. God created space, matter, time, and order making it possible for us to study and explain the complexity of life.

Jesus Christ is fully God and opposing him are empty philosophies like evolution that use deceit to replace the Truth and human tradition to undercut the worship of God Almighty. Instead of appreciating the wonders that God created for us to enjoy there are many who wish to supplant God's Glory with human theory and accidental creation. These academicians in white robes are like the Pharisees of old. God says, *"See to it that no one takes you captive by philosophy and empty deceit, according to human tradition, according to the elemental spirits of the world and not according to Christ for in Him the whole fullness of deity swells bodily."* The denial of truth has allowed the rise of dark forces drawing people to suicide, drug addiction, and bizarre sexual behavior.

Pornography is so widespread that it is the subject of one out of four Google searches. The devil is substituting God with empty man-made philosophy and perversion. The victims are millions upon millions of babies aborted and the youth which are being brainwashed. One study reveals that the average age that one sees porn is six and then sex-driven marketing in all media forms follows along as they grow up. These evil forces and dark powers are paving the way for a world rebellion and the Anti-Christ. It also promotes sex-trafficking and prostitution.

Will God decide to bring trials and judgment to a nation when it looks like more people are being taken down by evil than are being saved by faith? Contrast this with Daniel and his time. The kings had continuously disobeyed God, so God brought trials that affected the whole nation. Later when Daniel was a captive in Babylon, he faithfully obeyed God. God was able to work through him and in short time he was the King of Babylon's right-hand man. He interpreted Nebuchadnezzar's dreams connecting ancient empires to a future empire that will usher in the Anti-Christ. As we saw earlier, Daniel was given a prophecy that connects the degree of Cyrus the Great in 444- 45 BC to the exact day that Jesus made His Triumphal entry into the city of Jerusalem. Daniel's prophecy set the stage for the birth of the Savior and now has one more 7-year period to go. We could be approaching this end-time period now that Israel has been reestablished and the prophetic generation starting in 1947-48 has grown up. All the signs are converging in the *Crossroad.*

We would be wise to read and learn from the Book of <u>Daniel</u> and the entire Word of God and allow it to speak to us. Whether you believe it or not, God is orchestrating history with a divine order and deliberate intent to fulfill each of His Promises. Daniel was given a prophetic promise about the end-time generation that we are in. This promise may answer a mystery involving the church and the rapture, which were sealed for the future. He was told that this would be a time when knowledge would be increasing at a rapid rate and people would be moving rapidly. *"But you, Daniel, close up and seal the words of the scroll until the time of the end. Many shall run to and fro, and knowledge shall increase,"* Dan. 12:4.

This sounds like our modern world seen by Daniel about 2,500 years ago! The man who is dressed in white linen and gold has a body like beryl, which is clear like a diamond, and *"his face had the appearance of lightening, his eyes like flaming torches, and his words like the sound of a multitude!"* He tells Daniel what is inscribed in the "Book of Truth." This is probably a Christophany which is the pre-incarnate Jesus Christ. He tells Daniel to seal the message. Would Daniel's record of the vision help the Magi discover the baby Jesus? Will it also help us under the Sign of Revelation 12?

There are so many parallels between Daniel's time and our time that it seems obvious that there is a divine connection and that Daniel's 70th week is directly connected to God's Great Sign. This connection could be between both the extension of the prophetic 70-year generation to 80 years and to the 10 Days of Awe opening a window to a 10-year period of Mercy and Grace prior to this last 70th week and the Abomination of Desolation. God is giving the Church ample warning and He desires that we use this precious time to Speak the Gospel to the lost as the "Invisible Attack" shakes and weakens the world system.

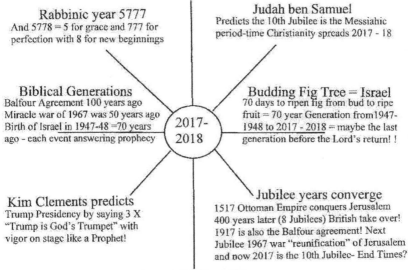

# The Divine Cross-Road !
## Gen.3:15
### Adam & Eve
Seed of Woman will crush Serpent's head
God names the Stars & Constellations-a Celestial clock
6000 years ago or 120 Jubilees. FIG leaf covers nakedness
Leo the Lion (of Judah) will crush head of the"Serpent" at the
heart is Regulus which is the brightest star at axis or center of
the earth's rotation- Jesus is the Center of Universe & world!

### Rabbinic year 5777
And 5778 = 5 for grace and 777 for
perfection with 8 for new beginnings

### Judah ben Samuel
Predicts the 10th Jubilee is the Messiahic
period-time Christianity spreads 2017 - 18

### Biblical Generations
Balfour Agreement 100 years ago
Miracle war of 1967 was 50 years ago
Birth of Israel in 1947-48 =70 years
ago - each event answering prophecy

**2017-2018**

### Budding Fig Tree = Israel
70 days to ripen fig from bud to ripe
fruit = 70 year Generation from1947-
1948 to 2017 - 2018 = maybe the last
generation before the Lord's return! !

### Kim Clements predicts
Trump Presidency by saying 3 X
"Trump is God's Trumpet" with
vigor on stage like a Prophet!

### Jubilee years converge
1517 Ottoman Empire conquers Jerusalem
400 years later (8 Jubilees) British take over!
1917 is also the Balfour agreement! Next
Jubilee 1967 war "reunification" of Jerusalem
and now 2017 is the 10th Jubilee- End Times?

### Rev. 12 / Sep.23
The Dragon awaits the birth of the Child
=Jupiter whose retrograde movement for 9
months represents birth pains in Virgo
with Leo, Sun, moon, and Stars aligned -
maybe first time since 6000 years ago!

Figure 4 above is an illustration of the Divine Crossroad which shows
8 different Divine signs crossing at year 2017-18: from God's Word
in the Fig Tree account to the Stars in heaven, to the Biblical

Generations and Jubilees, to the testimonies of men like Judah
Ben Samuel and Kim Clements, and to accounts in Genesis 3:15
and Revelation 12:1-4 (which represent the beginning and end of
time). This Divine *"Cross-Road"* is multi-dimensional. It mixes
God's prophetic promises given to Eve with those given Abraham,
Moses, and John the Apostle. The dragon appears in both Gen 3:15
and in Rev. 12:1-4, and the seed which is the child is both Jesus

Christ and the persecuted Church throughout history. God unfolds this prophecy and history in a time-pattern like Daniel's, leaving his footprints throughout.

We will see that the Fig Tree describes a last generation after the *budding* of the fig tree. It seems clear that the budding is the restored nation of Israel which was *born* in 1947-48. Add seventy years and it points to the Sign of the Woman in 2017. By studying Daniel, we see that God preserved a righteous remnant that 70 to 140 years later restored the Temple and the walls of Jerusalem. Is God going to save a righteous remnant today to face a coming trial? Does this mean we are heading for a great Revival or a soon to happen rapture?

All the Biblical generations point to our time, and it appears that God has been speaking prophetic truth to others including Ben Samuel and Kim Clements about our present time. The Jubilee year ends on Rosh Hashanah, September 20-22, 2017, and Daniel's Prophetic Generation that started in 1947-48 also ends on this date. As an important side note, this present Jubilee year began on the Day of Atonement in 1967, ten days after Rosh Hashannah. Note that Jubilee did not begin on Rosh Hashanah as does all the other 49 years; it begins on the Day of Atonement leaving behind 10 uncounted days for the new year, which are the 10 Days of Awe. Why are these 10 days not counted on God's clock or calendar for earth-time? Could this 10-day period represents the 10-year period of grace set aside for our generation?

The top and bottom intersecting lines, in Figure 4, reveals the amazing once in 6000-or-more year convergence of the Stars, moon, Jupiter and the three other planets. This is a celestial Time Wheel. The Feast days that follow were at the end of 40 days of repentance and represent God's Mercy and Love. This is significant for it lays out a progression of surrender after repentance, to a time of national atonement for sin, then a return to fellowship with God with an in-gathering of hope, and a promise of new beginnings. The Feast of Tabernacles is a time to recline and dine with God under the stars;

a special week to contemplate the future and discover ways to better honor and glorify God.

As we approach God's Feast Days we are drawn to wonder if God will again use them to fulfill an important part of his prophetic plan. Will He give us a period of grace if we repent and elect a righteous leader or if we humble ourselves and pray? This Divine Crossroad can be studied in the next chapter and with the next graph entitled, *The Cosmic Crossroad Chart* which will give a wider panorama of history and Jubilee periods so that you can understand God's footprints and His testimony relating to the rise and fall of people and of nations.

The Testimony of the Bible is our greatest authority. My book focuses on three of the most important books in God's Word for prophecy, theology, and historicity. Genesis, Daniel, and Revelation are the 3 most contested books in the Bible and therefore the most controversial. What is interesting is how important the opening of *Chapter 12* is in each of these books:

Chapter 12:1-3 of Genesis reveals the Promise of the SEED who will Bless all of mankind through Abraham. God told Abraham *"Get out of your country…to a land I will show you. I will make you a great nation; I will bless you… And in you all the nations of the world will be blessed."*

Chapter 12:1-3 of Daniel reveals a supernatural event that is reflected in the Revelation 12 account. *"At that time Michael shall stand up… and there will be a time of trouble such as never was a nation and of those who sleep in the earth will awake some to everlasting life. And those who turn many to righteousness will shine like the stars forever and ever."*

Chapter 12:1-3 of Revelation speaks of the Woman (Eve or Mary) who will give birth to the child (Jesus and the Church) both of whom will be persecuted by the Dragon with 7 heads and 10 horns. Then in verse 7 a war breaks out in heaven and *Michael* fights the *Dragon* who is then cast down to earth. The devil is then overcome by the blood of the Lamb and by the Word of the Testimony of the Saints – by their *righteousness.*

In Chapter 12:1-2 of Romans, a book that many consider to be the most important book on Christian theology; and the verses that reveal how to carry out and discover the will of God: *"Therefore, brothers by the mercies of God I urge you to present your bodies as a living sacrifice, holy and pleasing to God; this is your spiritual worship. Do not be conformed to this age, but be transformed by the renewing of your mind, so that you may discern the good, pleasing and perfect will of God."*

# CHAPTER FOUR

# The Biblical Generations Converge on the Jewish Year 2017-2018

In this chapter, we will investigate the meaning of the converging *Time Wheels* on the timeline of history. We will see how prophecy, Jubilee years, and the Generational years converge with this present age. We will study some of God's footprints in history and how they relate to our time including specific number sequences and special dates, parallel periods and other events in the Old and New Testament - including some of the great leaders and Prophets. One example is the Prophet Daniel. In the last chapter I discussed Daniel's *70-Weeks Prophecy* pointing forward to our time. Like Revelation 12 he had interchanges with Angelic beings and his vision into the future is also for this Day and Age.

God is measuring the end of the Age and He is going to use what we should call *Supernatural Time*, since only He knows the hour and the day. God, however, has given us a road map with road signs to guide us into the future. After all, Jesus castigated the expert Religion teachers and guides of His time by saying, *"Hypocrites! You know how to discern the face of the sky, but you cannot discern the signs of the times."* In writing this book I will take poetic license and call God's prophetic time sequences: *Prophetic Wheels of Time*. This could also be pictured as a spiral timeline as drawn on the cover of this book. The wheels would be more from man's viewpoint. Psalm 90:10, gives us a clue to God's plan. *"The years of our life are seventy, or even by reason of strength 80; yet their span is but toil and trouble; they are soon gone, and we fly away."*

Earlier we saw an important parallel message linking Genesis 3:15, and Revelation 12:1-4. The historical timeline shows that the time difference between the two dates is approximately 6000 years. There are many interesting parallels between the Old Testament and what God is doing in our present age. One important one is God's plan for the nation of Israel and the church. As we move into history, we will see a connection between the Jubilee years, the generational years, and prophecy. In Genesis 6:3 the Lord said, *"My Spirit will not contend with humans forever, for they are mortal; their days will be a hundred and twenty years."*

It is important to note that God's Spirit, which is the 3rd person of the Trinity, is active in trying to bring mankind to repentance. Just as with the Evangelists of today the Spirit ministered through the preaching of men like Noah and Enoch. Now, however, the Holy Spirit is sealed in the believer, and our salvation is guaranteed through Jesus Christ who is forewarning us that His plan will soon be fulfilled. He wants the church to get the message out to an unrepentant and disobedient generation. Not only are we called to be a witness to the lost, but we are to be a *living sacrifice,* an example to give hope in this last generation. God says, *"Obedience is better than sacrifice,"* but in this prophetic time He is also saying: *Obedience with sacrifice* is even better, since we do not have much time. The message of forgiveness and reconciliation is the best way to change hearts and to help us become God's voice. When Jesus died on the cross, He did it for all of us. We just need to believe to be justified. God canceled *"the record of debt that stood against us with its legal demands. He set it aside, nailing it to the cross,"* Col 2:14.

The Power of the Cross reconciles our debt or sin. He justifies us before the Judge. We will discuss this more in the next chapter.

I believe the statement, *"My Spirit will not contend with humans (the flesh) forever,"* relates to our generation, both Christians and non-Christians alike, and to the final tick on the Jubilee-Shemitah Time Clock which will be discussed in this chapter.

Jesus emphasized that the end time would be like Noah's time. He stated that their *"days will be a hundred and twenty years,"* before mankind faced Noah's flood. That was an extended time of Grace. God used water to cover the earth, to purify and not destroy it. The living would perish except for the *chosen* who were selected by God in pairs to enter the Ark. The shutting of the door of the ark represents the sealing of the Holy Spirit in us with the assurance of deliverance, and a Living Hope with New Beginnings. The New Beginnings would involve transformation from old to new. The new life brings new understanding and experiences. With Christ's resurrection there would be a new law measured by Grace written in the heart.

On Mount Sinai God wrote the Law with his own finger and instituted the Sabbath thus creating the WEEK as a measurement of time for work and rest. God set aside one 24-hour day a week, YOM in Hebrew, for us to rest and enjoy a relationship with Him. The word, "YOM," is the same word used to describe Day in Genesis Chapter one when God Almighty created all of Creation.

The Greatest Miracle of all time, the Creation of the Universe, was accomplished in six twenty-four-hour periods each delineated by the phrase *there was evening and there was morning* the first day and so on. Just as in Noah's time, people will scoff at believers in a supernatural God. Yes, God made the earth in 6 twenty-four days. They scoffed at Noah when he was building the ark on dry land. Today scoffers spew out a spiritual *"flood of sin"* as they attack God and Christians. And God will again judge the earth and those who dwell in it. They will miss the *Ark of Redemption* offered by the *Lord of Lords*, and *King of Kings*, Jesus Christ.

In Exodus 19:5, God promised his people as they entered the Holy Land, *"Now therefore, if you will indeed obey my voice and keep my covenant, then you shall be a special treasure to me above all people."*

Although God did not establish a covenant like that with America, He did establish our nation much like he did Israel. He brought persecuted people of faith through incredible hardship and helped them establish covenant communities. He then helped defeat adversaries that tried to suppress that freedom. A good example is the Pilgrim community which was founded on Bible based doctrines and principles. By divine chance they landed near fertile land and met a tribe-less Indian by the name of Squanto, whose tribe had perished years earlier and who spoke the English language. He became a liaison between other Indian groups and helped guide and prepare them for the winter.

Many of our founding fathers were Christians who were inspired to establish many seminaries that eventually became Ivy League Universities. Almost every signer of the Declaration of Independence professed a Christian faith, and many were pastors. All thirteen states had constitutions recognizing God as Creator. In the Revolutionary War and in the War of 1812, God seemed to have played a miraculous role in providing fog or storms to protect and deliver our weakened forces.

God seems to have preserved and protected America because of its Christian strengths and its eventual effort to help establish and defend the new nation of Israel. America is more deeply connected to modern and ancient Israel than any other country in the world. Rabbi Jonathan Cahn states, *"It can be argued that only two civilizations in history were established, dedicated, and consecrated to the will, the word, the purposes, and the glory of God from the moment of their conception."* The two would be Israel and America, and America is the first to support the people and nation of Israel. America also has the most effective mission system with extensive programs to feed the poor and help widows throughout the poor nations of the world. America's heart for ministry to even the most remote tribes has brought the Bible to countless lost people groups. Charities of every kind have treated the worst diseases and disasters and have given grief-stricken families hope. God is giving America and the lost world 10 years of Mercy.

Figure 5A & 5B in the next two pages gives a powerful linear perspective on history from the beginning of time to eternity in respect to God's carefully orchestrated footprints or markers. The symmetry of this chart shows one reason why we have reached the End of Days.

# COSMIC CROSSROAD CHART

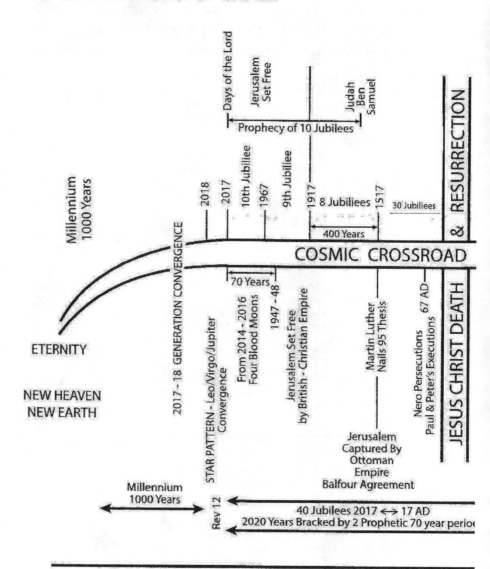

## Figure 5A & 5B

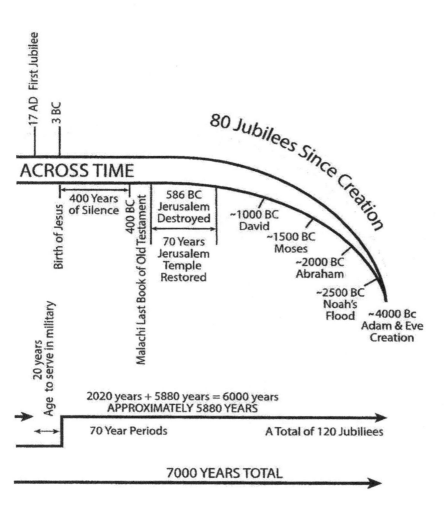

Figure 5 A & B shows history on a spiritual scale with God's Plan and promise surrounding Jesus Christ. There are many date sequences and periods that are interesting to study including the 70-week Daniel prophecy, the 70 years of exile in Babylon, and our 70-year prophetic generation starting in 1948-49.

This illustration will put into perspective much of what we have already discussed related to history and the date of the birth of Jesus, ancient and present-day Israel, prophecy and the Jubilees, special time spans such as the 400 and 1000-year periods, the blood moons and the beginning of time. We see that the Temple in Jerusalem was restored as promised in 70 years and soon afterwards there was 400 years of silence prior to the birth of the Jesus Christ in 3 BC. We see time divided into Jubilees and other important dates and so it would be wise to refer to this timeline as you read on.

This *Adam and Eve to Eternity Timeline Chart* shows a general progression of time with a series of *divine footprints* in both New and Old Testament times. Both have a 400-year and a 70-year period. In the New Testament we see dates correlating to major Jewish and Christian milestones. We can see Jubilee years playing a large role in the scale of events throughout, time before and after the birth of Jesus. At His birth, there is an interesting 20-year step from Old to New Testament years and covenants. This transition seems to go with the New Covenant God has established. There are 80 Jubilees looking back to Creation and 40 Jubilees pointing forward to this year. We can see the Sign of September 23rd, the date footprints of 1967 to 1947 and 1948 to 1917, and the interesting almost perfect series of steps-in-time in the Old Testament. Each step is about 500 years and continues for 2000 years. Those 80 Jubilees could print to 80-year Grace Period.

The Feast Days also fit into this dynamic picture of history orchestrated by God. Notice how the 2000-year periods of time balance in both Old and New Testament times with the birth of Jesus Christ at the center. Also note the blood moons and the timeline of Judah Ben Samuel's 10 Jubilee prophetic writing. The Jubilee years

seem to provide footprints in time around God's promises for Israel-
and the leaders who would change history to accommodate those
plans. There are two other important periods in Israel's history that
are close to 400 years. One relates to about 400 years that the Judges
ruled Israel, and the other is the 400 or more that the First Temple
existed - Solomon's Temple. These were periods of testing, building
up, and calling Israel to repentance. In most cases Israel failed until
God gave them a hero or prophet who would grant them a moment
of success or a prophetic word of hope. Likewise, God could be giving
us an extra 10 years.

On Mount Sinai God established the 7-day week and a 7- year
cycle for the people to observe. The seven-year cycle ended with a
year called the "Sabbath" or "Shemitah" (which means *Release*). God
declared: *"At the end of seven years you will make a release. And this
is the manner of the release: to release the hand of every creditor from
what he lent his friend; he shall not exact from his friend or his brother,
because the time of the release for the Lord has arrived,"* Deut. 15:1-2.
The last year of each seven-year period was to be set aside to redeem
the land and forgive debts. They were to leave the land fallow during
this full year. This was to honor God by showing Grace and Mercy
to those who will eat of the wild fruit and grain. It was a great benefit
to those who suffered loss. Just as the 7th day of the week was made
for a time of rest so would the 7th year be a year of rest for the land.

In this book we will call this 7-year period, *The Shemitah period*.
God also set aside one very special year every 50 years for man to
again honor Him by returning all land to its original owner. This
was to be called the *Jubilee Year*. The land was restored to the people
and the people to the land. This law would not only preserve the
boundaries and integrity of each tribe but would also protect anyone
dispossessed of their land including the widow and the orphan. A
series of 7 Shemitah periods is equal to 7 X 7 or 49. The final year
is the Jubilee year. The total period of 50 years is the Jubilee period.
The Shemitah after the first Jubilee period of this century ends in
2024-25. This period work mark time for God's redemption.

I realize that some theologians do not believe that these special periods are for today. They may not seem to have theological or spiritual import, but these time markers for return and release are still God's measuring tool for His divine timeline. This may be one reason why we see history moving in cycles and why we see divine interventions along the course of history especially in times of war. Examples are the extended fogs in preparation for the Allied invasion of northern Europe, and the evacuation of 8000 Revolutionary forces under George Washington from Brooklyn Heights. Other examples are storms that destroyed the Persian invasion force off the shore of Greece that sank the Spanish Armada off the coast of Ireland and England. Many do not know about the tornado-like storm that blew out the fires in Washington D.C. after the British set fire to the White House in 1812. That same storm stopped the British from advancing on Baltimore and eventually led to their defeat and retreat. Again, our nation was saved by weather! To fulfill His plan God will redeem people, nations, and even the earth storms and wars to fulfill His Promise.

He offers us His Grace as the free gift of Salvation. The fruit of this Grace is faith in God and the power of the Cross. How we live on this earth will determine how we spend eternity! God is interested in bringing as many people into his Kingdom as possible. Therefore, the shadow of God's Grace and the cross stretches back in time and is evident even in the Old Testament. Likewise, many of the traditions, tenants, and laws that God instituted in the Old Testament stretch forward into our time. Yes, we are no longer under the dictate of the Law for we are under Grace, but the message and lessons from this Old Testament vineyard is still with us today.In the last 74 years the vineyard has been transformed from a wasteland into the garden from which the gardener lovingly cultivates fruit. Will the final harvest come in soon?

According to the Torah the Jubilee year did not begin on Rosh Hashanah like a regular new year, but on Yom Kippur or The Day of Atonement. There is a 10-day Time-Gap where no time is counted!

This is the 10 Days of Awe and this delay for the new year occurs only just prior to the Jubilee year! It appears God was placing a "*little bit of heaven*" on earth a special, cube-like separation in the Temple called the *Holy of Holies*. Time is NOT counted for 10 days! God had a reason for this. Was it so that the Priests could account for sin in a real heaven- like sanctuary full of God's Grace and Holiness? The Holy of Holies after all has the same dimensions as the heaven that God promises us called the "*New Jerusalem.*" The cube-like dimensions are 15 X 15 X 15 or in the case of the city: 1500 X 1500 X 1500. There is only one other place in this Universe where Time is not counted. That one place is eternal Heaven where God dwells. The Creator of Time, Space and Matter, is not under the dictates of time, decay, sin, and death.

"*The house of the LORD was filled with a cloud, so that the priests could not stand to minister because of the cloud, for the glory of the LORD filled the house of God,*" 2 Chronicles 5:11 14.

On the Day of Atonement, the Trumpets are sounded throughout the land. The 40 days of repentance preceding the Day of Atonement and the 10 Days of Awe are all about preparing the heart, mind, and spirit for atonement and new beginnings. So, why is time not counted during the 10 Days of Awe in the Temple prior to the Jubilee year? Could it be because the Holy of Holies is Holy ground and God wanted the Priests to recognize that very fact? Could this *Holy silence* be related to the moment of silence between the 6th Seal and the 7th seal in Revelation? At this point seven angels are given 7 Trumpets, but do not blow them, and another angel comes to the altar with a golden censor and is given much incense to offer for the prayers of the Saints. At the Day of Atonement, the Priest with a golden censor and incense, offers prayers as he enters the Holy of Holies. The trumpets are not blown until after the Priest makes atonement for the sins of Israel. Are they following a pattern of God's Angels in Revelation 8 when the incense is gathered and thrown to earth opening the Trumpet Judgments? Is there a connection

63

here between Heaven and earth? Could what happens on earth be reflected by angels in heaven?

There is also a whole set of 7's, the Perfect Number, connecting the Holy of Holies with Heaven and Earth:

7 branches were in the golden candlestick (Exo. 25:37; Exo. 37:23);
7 times the blood was sprinkled on the day of atonement (Lev.16);
7 times the oil sprinkled upon the altar when it was consecrated;
7 days were required for consecrating the priests (Lev. 8:35);
7 days were necessary for purifying the defiled (Lev. 12:2);
7 times Naaman dunked himself in the Jordan (2 Kings 5:10);
7 days Jericho was besieged, and…
7 priests with 7 trumpets blew when the walls of Jericho collapsed
7 horns on the Lamb of God in heaven and seven eyes, which are the
7 spirits of God (Revelation 5:6);
7 seals are on God's book (Rev. 1:5) God also made the rainbow with
7 colors and the music scale with
7 notes to please the ear. We have 7 senses, 7 days in the week and there are 7 continents on earth. Seven is the *Perfect Whole*!

Normally during the 10 Days of Awe, on the morning of each day, the shofar is blown. This does not happen during the Jubilee year. <u>Could there have been a supernatural connection between heaven and earth on the Day of the Great Sign in relation to the beginning of the 10 Days of Awe</u>? Could this be magnified in heaven giving us an extra 10 years prior to the Abomination of Desolation which many believe will happen on the Day of Atonement? That could suggest that 2024-25 will initiate Daniel's 70th week and opening of the 1st Seal.

Would this *time of silence and prayer* reach the throne room in heaven and open the Door to Heaven? Ten days later, at the Day of Atonement God would meet with the High Priest just as he had met with Moses and Aaron in the Holy of Holies of the Tabernacle. Most scholars believe that He was the pre-incarnate Jesus Christ (the same

Christophany that Daniel saw) that was meeting with the High Priest and receiving the offering. The sacrifice would be consummated with the sprinkling of blood on the Ark of the Covenant in the Holy of Holies. This was a supernatural atonement, and therefore viewed and accepted by God as payment for the sin of the nation. Today even the simplest prayer given with the right heart is heard by God. This is because the Holy of Holies is in the *Temple of our Body* where the Holy Spirit dwells. When the rapture happens, we will meet with God.

We are in a spiritual sense God' s Holy nation. Peter says, *"But you are a chosen race, a royal priesthood, a holy nation, a people for his own possession, that you may proclaim the excellencies of him who called you out of darkness into his marvelous light."* 1 Peter 2:9.

Jesus says, *"If you ask anything in my name it shall be done."* And then he says, *"Yes, whoever continues to ask will receive. Whoever continues to look will find. And whoever continues to knock will have the door opened for them."* Luke 10:11.

It should be noted that in Chapter 7 of Revelation there is also an extended time of hesitation as the Angel from the East calls out to the 4 angels at the 4 corners of the earth not to harm the earth until the 144,000 are sealed from the 12 tribes. Immediately after this John sees a whole multitude of raptured saints. *"After these things I looked, and there was a crowd so large that no one was able to count it! They were from every nation, tribe, people, and language. They were standing in front of the throne and the lamb and were wearing white robes, with palm branches in their hands,"* Revelation 7. Is there a connection between the lost time in the Temple during the 10 Days of Awe and this divine hesitation in Revelation 7:1-8? It may be of no consequence. But again, we should remember the prayer taught us by Jesus himself, *"Thy Kingdom come, thy will be done on Earth as it is in Heaven."*

After the Day of Atonement there is a period of gathering of family and thoughts as one prepares for a new year of new beginnings. These five days are also used to collect tools and materials for the family to build the booth. They celebrate the Feast of Tabernacles outdoors with food and drink. This is the traditional time for the Jewish people to be under the stars with God as they were in the wilderness. Because of implications related to timing of the Sign in the stars and the Jewish feast days, I believe God may allow Israel a testing before the Feast of Tabernacles. The 5-day period between the Day of Atonement and the Feast of Tabernacles is called the *"Time of Gathering and New Beginnings."* The 40-day period of repentance has ended, and the 10 Days of Awe are now complete. The people have reconciled with God and with man. As stated earlier, this is now time for the families to gather, making promises and resolutions for the new year. Is it possible that this time of new beginnings will be one which God will gather and transform His church or the nation of Israel from the far reaches of the earth? Is this Feast gathering a reflection of the coming rapture? Does this also tie in with the period of silence noted earlier which would tie the rapture to Chapter 7 just after the great earthquake in Chapter 6?

The Jubilee ended just hours before the Sign of Revelation 12 happened when the year changed from 5777 to 5778. When the sequence of 7 Shmita periods or 49 years came to an end in 2017 the 50th year or Jubilee year began. It ended in 2018 and a new 7-year Shmita period started which will end in 2025. It is the first in a new 50-year period and could represent a period of Grace and purification.

In his book, The Mystery of the Shemitah, Jonathan explains how the Shemitah year has forecast major downturns in the American economy! The parallels are stunning and suggest that they are linked to God's *spiritual time* and a Shemitah type judgment. He then goes on to explain that the Jubilee year is a Super Shemitah. Every seventh year was the Sabbath Year or the Shemitah and every seventh Shemitah, or 49th year, was followed by the Super Shemitah or the Jubilee year. Is the 2017-18 Jubilee foreshadowing God's judgment? Everything including winds, fires, and other trials are intensifying. Each new election has generated more fear, chaos, and uncertainty. The world sees us as being weaker and divided. Economies worldwide

COSMIC CROSSROAD COUNTDOWN

have been weakened by Covid-19 and other invisible forces. All of this was predicted by the Great Sign. God is in control, and He will direct our future.

The promises and prophetic messages in the books of <u>Daniel</u> and <u>Isaiah</u> should answer any doubts that the Jews have. They should understand that Jesus is the suffering servant who died for their sins – "*for all of us, like sheep have gone astray.*"

For the last 2000 years the Jubilee has not been officially celebrated. Then in September of 2015, the Sanhedrin of Israel officially declared the restoration of the Jubilee. The Sanhedrin, or Bet din (rabbinic court), ruled that enough Jews have returned to inherit the land as a nation. So, the Jubilee Year is now an official measure of spiritual time and law in Israel and for all Jews everywhere. I used the term *spiritual* here because it is not the official law of the land just like *getting drunk* is not illegal in the courts, but it is against God's spiritual Law. For the sake of measuring time let us also consider the importance of the Jubilee year that was to be set aside every 49 years in Israel. If the age of the earth is 6000 years this would make the clock tick 120 Jubilee years: 120 X 50 = 6000, refer to Figure 5.

Because the Jubilee year is a special year set aside by God, many call it a Holy Year. Could it be God's timekeeper to judge righteousness or faithfulness in other nations like America. We are a nation founded on the Bible and those who wrote our Constitution were mostly strong Christians? Is God still judging spiritual Israel based on the Jubilee year? Israel paid the penalty for 10 of those Jubilee years during their exile in Babylon and Persia. Because Israel broke God's Laws those 10 Jubilee years, according to Levitical law, were multiplied by 7 to equal 70 penalty years. That equals the time of the Babylonian exile. Are the Jews who live outside of Israel in a self-imposed exile? God wants them to return to His Promised land.

Israel has helped nations throughout the world and has been responsible for advances in every field of science and the fine arts. They have won more Nobel prizes per capita than any other nation. Yet, they have one of the highest per capita rates of abortion and of porno-based sex use in the world. They have a powerful military, but does this make them less dependent on God? At one-point King David felt very self-confident and took a census of his soldiers, then God dealt with his sin by bringing a plague that killed 70,000 Israelites. God does not want his spiritual leaders, nor His Chosen people to rely on their own laurels or strength nor on the approval of others.

Are we being judged by Israel's standard? Maybe not directly, but we do know that whatever happens to Israel will affect the whole world. Right now, God has reason to judge the rebellious Jew and to draw other Jews from the global network of Synagogues back to Israel. How will He do this? He may have to shake up the nations to draw His people back. God has gifted his people with so much talent. We know how God has blessed them in the creative arts, music, and film, yet how many of them have given God the Glory? How many totally turned away from the God of their fathers? Many have expressed their disdain for Christians, the Bible, the Cross, and for their homeland, Israel.

And many Christians are guilty of this too. In fact, a recent Barna poll indicates that only 17 percent passed a simple quiz on Christian doctrine and belief. On the cover of a recent *Newsweek* magazine the title declared, *The Decline and Fall of Christian America.* A recent article pronounced, *8 Evangelical Leaders Who Publicly Embrace Apostasy!* So, when is God's patience going to expire? The answer will catch many by surprise. The next question goes to the heart. Are you more concerned about the approval of man over the approval of God? Take a real hard look and do a deep spiritual inventory. Most people cannot see their own lies because they have been living behind a wall of lies for so long. Only Jesus Christ can take down those walls and expose them to the Light. Do it soon! Jesus said, *"On this rock I will build my church and the gates of Hell will not prevail against it."*

When we add the 1000-year Millennium to the 6000 years, we are at the Total Age of 7000 years, or the *Perfect Age* of the Earth! The 6000 years are years of *work* and the final 1000 is the *Sabbath*

*Century* of *rest*. God established the Shemitah as a year of rest for the land and the forgiveness of debts called the *Lord's release*. Jubilee on the other hand means *Liberty or Release* and required the land to be returned to its original owner. Even kings and the priests were not to dispossess people of their land. As stated earlier it is a *Holy Year*. The land was the foundation of God's promise to Israel: *The Promise Land*.

In the end man will be held accountable to God for sins committed and the land will be refined by fire to create a new Earth. There is a time span or measure maintained by God for the earth and the universe to be determined by the number of saints martyred, and/or the spread of the Gospel throughout the earth. As soon as that number is achieved, He will open the last seal judgment which will release them all. Some believe that none of the seals can take effect until the last binding is released. John the Apostle reports, "*The Lamb opened the fifth seal. Then I saw some souls under the altar. They were the souls of those who had been killed because they were faithful to God's message and to the truth they had received.* These souls shouted in a loud voice, "*Holy and true Lord, how long until you judge the people of the earth and punish them for killing us? Then each one of them was given a white robe. They were told to wait a short time longer...*" Rev. 6:9-11.

Time is obviously a key element in any convergence. We shall see how carefully God measures and appoints time! Discussing anything related to the rapture raises issues. I do want to make sure that I allow the Holy Spirit to teach me and guide me in Truth. This next chart shows a convergence of Wheels of Time on a timeline leading to today.

The linear time which has a beginning at Creation intersects either a prophetic Wheel of Time, a celestial wheel of time, or a testimonial wheel of time. They generate markers that point us forward to a prophetic promise that is about to be fulfilled. God has appointed a different *wheel of time* to measure the day, the year, and the end of the Age. To measure the end of the Age He is going to use what we should call *"supernatural"* time since only He knows the dates.

The child that we saw in Revelation 12 is both Jesus Christ and the church. They are interconnected in prophecy with the church being a mystery in the Old Testament but fulfilled in the New Testament. It is important to understand that the *child* does not determine when the rapture happens! The child or church is being persecuted now and it has been pursued by Satan for the last 2000 years. We should realize that just because things in America are fine, it does not mean that the church elsewhere is not being persecuted. The media has spent so much time and effort pursuing senseless topics to where people do not know how bad off the entire populations are in places like Africa. *Open Doors, Samaritan's Purse, The Jesus Film Project,* and other global ministries provide detailed accounts of what is happening to the church worldwide.

These are widespread physical and spiritual attacks against the church worldwide. These assaults on Christianity are increasing and despite persecution the Chinese agenda will continue to accelerate through missions and ministries on the airwaves. The Word of God has reached remote tribes through ministries like Wycliffe and other Bible translators. Many who cannot read nor write are being saved through dreams and visions in which Jesus Christ has appeared to them. God is on the move in a big way and many who are lost are seeing revival in their families and in their land.

Could the media attacks lead to a backlash that will cause a national crisis or could persecution and severe weather conditions result in a worldwide crisis? Or will this be a time of revival in America? Jesus Christ warned us about birth pains, including a coming lawlessness. He said, *"Many will come in my name and say, 'I am the Messiah, 'and they will deceive many people. You are going to hear of wars and rumors of wars. See to it that you are not alarmed. These things must take place, but the end hasn't come yet, because nation will rise up in arms against nation, and kingdom against kingdom. There will be famines and earthquakes in various places. But all these things are only the beginning of the birth pains. They will hand you over to suffer and will kill you, and you will be hated by all the nations because of my name. Then many people will fall away, will betray one another, and will hate one another. Many false prophets will appear and deceive many people, and because lawlessness will increase, the love of many people will grow cold. But the person who endures to the end will be saved. And this gospel of the kingdom will be proclaimed throughout the world as a testimony to all nations, and then the end will come."* Mat., 24:5-14

We have seen how important our present Jubilee is, which some call a Holy Jubilee. This is because it is the first Jubilee of the century and thus may have special significance. This does ring true, since most of the major Jubilees discussed in this book were the first of their century. Most of the major Jubilees discussed in this book were the first of their century. We have seen how God's timeline includes *"wheels of time"* that focus on distinctive events. The Jubilee periods, the stars, and the prophetic generations are spiral calendars or clocks in themselves that register as *wheels of time.* Their *sets of time* focus on a distinct date like a magnifying lens, drawing our attention to patterns or steps in history. These *clocks* give us a pattern in God's plan for redemption and a fulfilling of his promises and prophecy. The *wheels* are not eternal, whereas the timeline or spiral line is. Refer to figure #6. The wheels of time draw us to those distinctive dates on the timeline as they converge one-upon-the-other. Two wheels not present are Daniel's 70-week prophecy and the 80-year new beginning period. When they converge with the other wheels the convergence is complete.

My concern is that Israel will be the center of the next major trial on this earth. And if there is an early rapture, my thought is that less than half the worldwide church will be gathered to meet Christ in the clouds. This is reflected in the parable of the 10 Virgins where only 5 have the oil of a salvation, the light of the Holy Spirit and Jesus Christ. The rest will face trials or tribulation! God may be interested in refining the church first by the *fire* of testing and trials as he did the Jewish remnant during the 70 years of captivity in Babylon and Persia. He provides a remnant deliverance with the restoration of Jerusalem.

A wilderness experience happened as the nation was born out of Mount Sinai. Although I favor the pre-tribulation rapture, a tribulation like we are seeing in many 3rd world countries could happen here, especially since we are seeing so much rebellion in hearts of people and the media. We need to keep out nation and our people and the media. We need to keep our Christian leaders and other people in authority in prayer since judgment will come down harder on them.

The first person to recognize Jesus as the Son of God, was not Peter, it was Nathaniel who was sitting under the *fig tree*, John 1:48. The first words out of Nathaniel's mouth were, *"How could anything good come out of Nazareth?"* In just a matter of minutes he went from total skepticism (like the behavior of the nation of Israel) to total devotion after realizing that Jesus could see through distance, time, and the heart. Many Jews will believe and cry out *"Blessed is he who comes in the name of Lord,"* when Jesus sets foot in a miraculous way on the Mount of Olives.

Hopefully, you will not need to see Jesus Christ to believe. And do not put your trust in evolution, a created angel-type of Jesus Christ, or a spiritualized Book of Revelation. God reveals Truth and has the answer to all Questions, after all the book of Colossians says, *"All the treasures of wisdom and knowledge are found in Christ Jesus!"* By the way, this wisdom is not found in a secular science class. Parents have given up their kids to a school system that is eager to steal away their faith in God and their innocence. The media and educational institutions are substituting good for evil and evil for good in the classroom and online. Poland is called a repressive country for limiting immigration, African nations are called suppressive regimes because they have Christian leadership that limit abortion or homosexuality, despite spiraling rates of HIV and other sexual diseases. America has become the biggest purveyor of pornography, violent film and games, pharmaceutical drugs, and gambling in the world. When God sees that we are thwarting the efforts of other countries in the advancement of the Gospel, He may bring judgment. As God sees children and Christians being so affected by evil, He may rapture the Church.

If indeed God wants to discipline the church and purify the saints, He will allow a period of tribulation before the Day of the Lord. Both Joel in Joel 2:31, and Peter in Acts 2:20, state, *"The sun shall be turned into darkness, and the moon into blood, before the great and terrible Day of the Lord comes." This begins what is called "the Last Days."* Then Revelation 6:12-17, states, *"Then I saw Him open the sixth seal. A violent earthquake occurred; the sun turned black like sackcloth made of goat hair; the entire moon became like blood; the stars of heaven fell to the earth as a fig tree drops its unripe figs—the sky separated like a scroll being rolled up; and every mountain and island was moved from its place."* How interesting that God again uses the *Fig Tree* as an analogy and is this an indirect reference to something happening to an unrepentant Israel, or an Israel that is caught by surprise.

The earthquake in the 6th Seal is so massive that it shakes and moves every island and mountain on earth. Some *Mid-Trib* advocates believe that this earthquake is caused by the worldwide rapture as graves crack open. They parallel this to the Resurrection of Jesus Christ when there was a large earthquake and people were raised from the dead. Joel stated that the sack-cloth sun and the blood moon occur right before the *Day of the Lord*. In contrast the blood moon and darkened sun in the 6th Seal of Revelation happen in the middle of the 7- year Tribulation. So, how does the *Pre-Trib* advocate explain this? Most will admit that there must be two blood moons with a darkened sun.

God loves to humble the self-proclaimed expert or genius. If you are one, I ask you to answer three simple questions: 1) If the earth was a ball of fire and it now has billions of trillions of gallons of water, where did all that water come from? 2) We now know that even the cell of an amoeba has such a complex DNA code and metabolism system that outperforms the most sophisticated computer run robots or submersibles of today-it can even replicate itself and heal itself! So how did the amoeba's information system evolve; do computer systems evolve; does language evolve? 3) How does an explosion turn into an ordered environment or go from nothing to something?

I will admit that as an intelligent and well-educated doctor, I was brainwashed and believed in evolution until I met Truth. Brains can be fooled quite easily as we demonstrate by using 2 rhomboid shaped color swatches that make the red one look much bigger than the other. When laid one upon the other people are shocked to see that they are of equal size. Likewise, most men think heated aluminum foil will burn hands - guess what - it does not. We are often deceived because we think that we are smart and are therefore full of pride. God will humble us, just wait!

Revelation 6:12-17 states, *"Then the kings of the earth, the nobles, the military commanders, the rich, the powerful, and every slave and free person hid in the caves, and they said, 'Fall on us and hide us from the face of the one seated on the throne and from the wrath of the Lamb because the great day of their wrath has come!'"* Some who associate the rapture to this earthquake believe these leaders of the world will fall on their faces with shame and fear as they witness their loved ones and Christian servants disappear. As stated earlier, Joel 2:32 states these events come before the *Day of the Lord*. Does this mean that the Seal judgments all happen before the time of great tribulation or the *Day of the Lord*? Does this mean that the Seal judgments all happen before that time of great tribulation? After the 6th Seal, the Apostle John, speaks of the same *four winds* that Jesus speaks of in Matthew 24:31, *"He will send out His angels with a loud trumpet, and they will gather His elect from the four winds, from one end of the sky to the other."* Does the rapture of the Church therefore happen after these six Seal judgments? I pray not. Hopefully, God raptures the Church before the chaotic Seal judgments.

Know that God has reconciled the world to himself, and He eagerly awaits each heart and mind that chooses to have a relationship with him. God reconciled us, *"By canceling the record of debt that stood against us with its legal demands. This he set aside, nailing it to the cross,"* Col 2:14. God has a record of all our sin, and He cancels it the minute you trust in the Blood of Jesus Christ. All sin is *"placed under the Cross,"* where it was reconciled. For all who trust in the power of the Cross, the blood of Christ justifies them in the eyes of God. God views us from Heaven like he viewed the *"Cross in the Wilderness,"* we are all part of His plan for Redemption and destined to come under the power of the Cross. He sends the hounds of heaven after us and watches over us to draw us to Him. All we need to do is accept the sacrifice that He made on the Cross for us.

The Crossroad of prophetic events and signs point to the cross and what it stands for. The Church is called to point the world to Jesus Christ. Our weapon is not of this world, *"For we do not wrestle against flesh and blood, but against the rulers, against the authorities, against the cosmic powers over this present darkness, against the spiritual forces of evil in the heavenly places,"* Eph. 6:12. Do you believe that the Voice of God can speak to anyone? Do you think that your pastor would listen to you if God did speak to you?

Speak to you and the Holy Spirit guides you?

Are you prepared for a big storm? We are being taken over by a meta-generation with a meta-world of meta-technology that is creating its own gods and reality. The youth feel empowered by this virtual reality where they can experience the past, the future, or any location on earth with the push of a button. Many are already willing to give up real Truth, real Freedom and real Love for this fake reality. The storm that we may soon see will evolve from this deceptive reality with its lies.

It is a dark pyramid of evil, representing 666 or 3 conjoined equilateral triangles from a Principality of ancient Evil. These dark forces are waiting as they prepare the stage for the anti-Christ. They worship the dark power and spirit that comes with it. God is giving us signs of its coming, like the Sign of Revelation 12 and the warnings in Matthew 25 and from prophets like Joel: *'And I will show wonders in the heavens and on the earth, blood and fire and columns of smoke. The sun shall be turned to darkness, and the moon to blood, before the great and awesome day of the LORD comes.'"* Joel 2:29-31. Are you prepared for the perfect storm that will ensue when Satan is cast out of heaven with his angels? Before this happens, we will see the earth's birth pains where both physical elements and invisible agents will cause sever havoc.

*"Then I heard every created being that is in heaven and on earth and under the earth and in the sea, everything in all these places, saying, 'All praise and honor and glory and power forever and ever to the one who sits on the throne and to the Lamb!"* Rev. 5:13. Many Christians believe that these are the raptured Saints in heaven, and those mentioned in Chapter 7 are the Saints saved during the great tribulation.

What is important is to trust in God and His plan for Salvation and eternity. The following verses make it clear that there is a rapture of believing Christians: 1) Mat. 24:30 states, *"The Sign of the Son of Man will appear in the sky, and then all the peoples of the earth will mourn; and they will see the Son of Man coming on the clouds of heaven with power and great glory. He will send out His angels with a loud trumpet, and they will gather His elect from the four winds, from one end of the sky to the other;"* 2) then Paul states in I Cor. 15:52, *"In a moment in the twinkling of an eye, at the last Trumpet, the trumpet will sound, and dead will be raised incorruptible, and we will be changed."* Both speak of a trumpet sound that may be one and the same. and the same. These verses assure the Saints that they will be raptured before the Day of the Lord. 1ˢᵗ Thess. 5:9, says that we are no *"appointed unto wrath."* One more key reason to trust in the rapture is found in the book of Acts 1:9-11, where the Angel tells those who looking up in bewilderment, as Jesus ascends to heaven, to not be concerned *"For He, Jesus Christ, will return in the same way that he left."* Therefore, even the angels confirm that Jesus will come back in the clouds!

The *child* in our Revelation 12:1-3 sign, is the Church or believing Jews. 1) The *child* will be be pursued by the *dragon* then will be caught up. This phrase "caught up" is the Greek word

*"Harpatzo"* or the Latin word *"Rapturo"* which is the same word used in Thessalonians 4:17 concerning the church: *"Then we who are still alive will be caught up together with them in the clouds to meet the Lord in the air; and so we will always be with the Lord."* 2) Jesus was not raptured, nor did he ever need to be rescued since He is God, therefore the child is more likely the church. This truth is part of the blessing promised by God.

Just like the Fig Tree lesson this aspect of Prophecy presents the reader with a riddle that he must investigate to get the blessing of Truth revealed through the Word of God and the Holy Spirit. The Book of Revelation is the only Book that promises a Blessing to the one who reads or hears it with understanding. It is also the only Book that promises a *curse* if anything is added or subtracted from it. So, if someone teaches Revelation in error will they be cursed? By the way the Lord has blessed me ever since I wrote these books. As explained earlier the combination of the following signs points to a divine event sometime in the near future: 1) *The Revelation 12 Sign* at Rosh Hashanah, 2) the end of the Jubilee, 3) the end of the 70-year generation spoken by Jesus in the Olivet Discourse, 4) the 3½ year templates, 5) the connection to all the important generational periods, 6) the Solar Eclipse, 7) and of course the amazing convergence of all these signs in a short period of time. Does it all point to the end?

Deuteronomy 4:29, *"But if from thence thou shalt seek the LORD thy God, thou shalt find him, if thou seek him with all thy heart and with all thy soul."* God desires our heart, soul, and spirit." Zechariah 12:3, *"And in that day I will make Jerusalem a burdensome stone for all people: all that burden themselves with it shall be cut in pieces, though all the people of the earth be gathered together against it."* The god of this age has blinded leaders and the nations will pay for transgressions against Israel. They will fail to know the time and see God's Sign of the end. This is a great example of the Gentile connection to the Jewish *Time Wheel.* Is America being being weighed by how we treat the nation of Israel?

The *Wheel of Jubilees* is important because God ordained the Jubilee year to be a time of Forgiveness, Reconciliation, Restoration, Return, and for Grace and Divine Justice. Because the nation of Israel did not follow God's command for the approximate 10 Jubilees of their nation building, God brought their destruction and then exiled them for 70 years. Mt. Sinai, and He is forewarning us in this period of new beginnings and uncertainty.

Four times in Leviticus God says, "*I will strike you sevenfold for your sins*" and 10 Jubilees X 7 = 70 years. There is one other way to calculate 70 years of judgment, if one calculates that Israel was nation building for 490 years instead of 465 years. This would include the period that Samuel was Judge - a man who was chosen by God to warn the people and appoint or remove the King. Earlier we saw how Shemitah or the Sabbath year is the 7th year, a time which God set aside for Israel to forgive debts and leave the ground fallow. A series of 70 Sabbath years not honored by the kings and people would leave Israel again, with a debt to God of at least 70 years (7 X 70 Sabbath years = 490 years).

In Review: The 70-year prophetic generation plays a big part in the history of Israel. We will see how it also plays a big part in Daniel's vision. There is a supernatural connection between the 10 Days of Awe, and wheels of time involving Jubilee years, Prophecy, and both Gentile and Jewish time from God's Omniscient view. Everything on the timeline has a purpose in relation to the Revelation 12 Sign. The 10 Days of Awe suggest that the normal measure of time will depend on God's Grace. There will be a series of events related to the Invisible attack which will lead us to Daniel's 70th week. As we have seen with Fractals and the Fibonacci ratios, sequenced numbers are God's way of keeping order and design in His creation. There will be a pattern related to 10 years which will add to the 70 to equal 80.

The Israelites had to pay the price with a 70-year hiatus: Deut. 28:62-63, "*You who were as numerous as the stars in the sky will be left but few, because you did not obey the Lord your God. Just as it pleased the Lord to make you prosper and increase in number, so it will please*" *him to ruin and destroy you. You will be uprooted from the land you are entering to possess.*" Will America as a nation deserve judgment for not honoring God in the education of children and for not seeding the Word of God in their hearts? We have put our children in a dark hole of sin and confusion. We have already aborted millions of others! This historical Biblical account shows that God does take His warnings and promises very seriously. In the next few pages, we will see an exciting correlation between 80, 70, 50, and 40 years

Hebrews 3:7-10: "*So, as the Holy Spirit says: 'Today, if you hear his voice, do not harden your hearts as you did in the rebellion, during the time of testing in the desert, where your fathers tested and tried me and for forty years saw what I did. That is why I was angry with that generation, and I said, 'Their hearts are always going astray, and they have not known my ways.'*"

Year 2017 was a Jubilee year and therefore important to events in prophecy. As we saw earlier the Jubilee begins after the end of the 49th year which ends on Rosh Hashanah. Year 2017-18 was a Jubilee year itself did not start until The Day of Atonement. There is a missing gap of time that is not accounted for. This gap encompasses the 10 Days of Awe including both Rosh Hashanah and the Day of Atonement. During the 10 Days of Awe, the High Priest would remember the sins of the nation offering incense and prayers to the LORD. Since time was not counted it might be considered a sinless vacuum or void in sin's contamination. In today's world there is no longer a sacrifice nor a temple, but those 10 days are a reminder for remorse, reconciliation, restitution, and return. Recently much of what our nation's leadership has done is corrupt and there has NOT been any Return to God. Those 10 days have been magnified into 10 years where God has extended His Mercy prior to the Abomination of Desolation. This abomination will occur on the Day of Atonement in 2027-28. The 10 years are for the Salvation of the lost. Subtracting 3 ½ years we get 2024-25 as a time for the storm and other events to magnify as it leads to anti-Christ.

Tradition says that the Sabbath that occurs during 10-Day period has God writing His Book on everyone, and with prayer, repentance, and fasting a person can *Change the Books*. Those are the books on which God registers a person's deeds. One 3rd century rabbi wrote, *"Three books are opened in heaven on Rosh Hashanah, one for the completely wicked, one for the completely righteous and one for those in between. The completely righteous are immediately inscribed in the book of life. The completely wicked are immediately inscribed in the book of death. The fate of those in between is suspended until the Day of Atonement."* And others during the 40-day period prior to the Day of Atonement called Teshuva. Ask your Jewish friends about this period. Therefore the Jews prefer to do business only among themselves.

The 50-year Jubilee period includes 7 Shemitah periods or Sabbath years of 7 years each or 7 X 7 = 49 years. Note that the 49th year is a Sabbath year at which time the Israelites were supposed to leave the ground fallow and forgive debts and free the bond servant. As stated before, the Jubilee year followed the protocol requiring forgiveness of debts, freedom, and keeping the land fallow. But it also included the Return of the Land to the original owners. God promised the people that He would give a special blessing of crops on the 7th year of each Shmita period. Since they were not to plant on that year nor on the Jubilee year, the Jewish farmer needed 3 years of harvest in one year every 50th year. This was a good example of God's Grace in the Old Testament. This was grace multiplied and applied in a way to sustain his people and temper the legalism of the leaders. It would make the whole nation dependent on God's laws and grace in a harsh time. Widows and the elderly were allowed to glean of the wild fruit and grain, thus giving them a way to survive.

Thus, we can see how God instituted Grace into the Law and into the lives of his people. He also instituted the Jubilee to assure the integrity of the family, the tribe, and the nation. Likewise, on the Holy Jubilee he held The Priest accountable to the unique <u>Special 10-day Period of Awe</u>. Was this *period of awe* meant to remind the

COSMIC CROSSROAD COUNTDOWN

nation and the Priest that God was going to provide 3 years of food and sustenance while their land was not producing for three years? Was it a special time of AWE because God was making sure that his people put their trust in Him, and not to let fear or doubt dictate their lives? YES, and YES. This is key to understand why the Sign of Revelation 12 fell on the beginning of those 10-Days and why it is so Important. It will MARK the last 10 YEARS for God's Provision of Grace and Mercy with Great Miracles to bring the LOST into His fold.

The Jubilee year also interconnects with the prophetic 70-year, and the 20-year periods that bracket the *Messianic* age. We will understand this better in the explanation of figures 5 and 6. The 1st Jubilee in the 20th century came right after World War I and saw Jerusalem released from the control of the Ottoman Empire. The first Jubilee of the 21st century is this year and happens during a Teshuvah (40 days of Repentance) that coincides exactly with the major Solar Eclipse in America - which is described in Chapter 3. Historically when a Repentance Solar Eclipse happens there has been a period of great revival: *The First and Second Great Awakenings, Azusa Street Revival*, and Charismatic Revival. The new revival will be worldwide and will involve those who have little hope and will include refugees from war, disasters, and evil dominions. The church will be called to help and rescue these people who will see dreams and visions and others who will flee to safety in America and the Western Powers. God is drawing them to Him.

Christian crusades have brought revival to countries as far away as South Africa and Australia. Revival is spreading! However, Africa, India, Central America, and the Middle East may continue to suffer from corruption or severe drought. Many of these countries have leaders that are being paid off by the Chinese government or are involved in either drug or slave trades. This has led to tribal disputes, gang wars, or a deepening spiritual darkness. For this reason, I believe they have lost God's blessing, and many suffer for it. This includes South Africa and any nation that abuses the trust of its people. The world is enduring long protracted regional conflicts, with Christian and Jewish persecution throughout the Middle East. The eyes of God are upon us and upon the nations as the shadow of Revelation 12 is cast over the World.

It was during the last part of a 50-day revival that I traveled to South Africa, Swaziland, and Namibia. Inspired by the Holy Spirit and trained by *Time to Revive*, I felt a real need and desire to share the Gospel wherever I went. On my second day in Cape town, I decided to walk back from the harbor and ended up at the wrong Protea hotel. Believing that God had a purpose in this I started sharing the Gospel in their beautiful plaza area. I asked one lady if she knew Jesus Christ and with eyes wide open, she said, *"You know just minutes ago I was thinking of sharing the Gospel."* I then asked her if she wanted to share the Gospel with me and within minutes, we led a lost soul to the Lord. She then had to catch the train home, so I proceeded on my own seeking to find my hotel.

This next part reads like <u>Pilgrim's Progress</u>. As I was trying to decide which fork in the road to take a bedraggled man approached, asking if I needed some help. He told me told his name was "Good Man." I asked him about the location of my Protea hotel, and he said, *"Let me show you the way."* As he walked ahead of me, two men moved in from the side, motioning Good Man to leave, then telling me that I could not go the way we were headed. I asked, *"Why not?"* And followed with, *"Where are the road blockades?"* Then 2 more men came in from the opposite side and said that it was true, that I could not proceed down the road. They insisted that I detour down a side path. Then a fifth man came from the direction that we had been headed, and he was wearing the typical roadworker's reflective vest. He stated, *"You cannot proceed down the road without a permit."*

I grew up in the streets of Fortaleza, Brazil, Maracaibo, Venezuela and Laredo, Texas. I know the *way of the street* and so remained calm - plus I knew that God was with me. So, as the men tried to convince me that I needed to go with them I just said, *"My friend is waiting for me just up the street"* and pointed in the direction that I had been going. When these five men all turned to look, I just walked through them and *me, and he can deliver you."* He appeared around the corner trembling in fear as he had been severely threatened. I shared the Gospel with him, saying, *"God can deliver you just as he has delivered me."* Good Man accepted God's invitation and I gave him a Bible and a "Time to Revive" bracelet. During the entire time, Good Man did not ask for money, so I asked him to tell me about his life. After he shared, I gave him some money and prayed for him. Before leaving on this trip, I had felt directed to give away not only the Gospel, but also money to the outcasts and street people. I continue to pray for these people and for these countries that are suffering under poor leadership. Can we now expect a wave of revival in America, or conversely a new time of trial and tribulation?

Light and darkness are at war in every aspect of life in our world system. The world is seeing drug and nuclear proliferation, and an increase in violence of every kind, worldwide terrorism, disrespect for authority, crazed detestable acts, volcanic activity, famines, and earthquakes. Ironically, countries like Russia and the Philippines that have been excoriated by the press are allowing Bibles and Bible studies in their public schools. Whatever happens, God will reign and will judge the nations after Daniel's 70th week. Like the *"Lost Generation" in the wilderness of Arabia, we are under the watchful eye of God*! Those who experience severe trials need to walk in faith and persevere, placing their Trust in God! God will provide, *"For you are my Rock and my Fortress, you lead me and guide me, ...you are my refuge into your hand I entrust my spirit; you redeem me, LORD, God of Truth,"* Psalm 31 of David.

The wheels of time discussed in figure 6, also have both a Gentile and a Jewish path. And as will be discussed later, there are supernatural *Wheels of Time* overlapping both. The supernatural ones include the prophetic timelines. These wheels intersect the timeline forming a supernatural crossroad and possibly a period of Grace provided by God before the final End-time 7-year countdown. This is different than what Ezekiel saw as heavenly Wheels with eyes surrounding the throne. Throne. This is discussed further in Chapter 8.

Do those eyes watch over us and await our repentance? Do they oversee Prophecy and the fulfillment of God's promises? We know that God watches over us and has throughout history brought storms and other severe trials against certain leaders, nations, and empires. God seems committed to prevent dark forces from interfering with His plans to preserve a remnant and save the Lost. Drugs like fentanyl are killing more people than ever with over 100,000 dying this year alone. Trafficking and other crimes against children are rising at alarming rates.

Will God intervene against superpowers like China and Russia who are threatening their neighbors and the entire world? America's failure in Afghanistan has motivated Europe to rethink their alliances and to consider forming a one-Europe army. All that is required is for a charismatic leader take control. Many countries have already imposed Draconian police powers over the people. These intrusions and the fall of economies has crippled many small businesses and farms. Soon inflation and shipping problems will cripple them more allowing Big Corporations to take more control.

The fall of the dollar will further weaken America in the eyes of the world. People often forget that America's power comes from "Goodwill" and when this falters America will discover that its debt is unsustainable. American does not have much time before it loses its superpower status and has to humble itself.

# WHEELS OF TIME

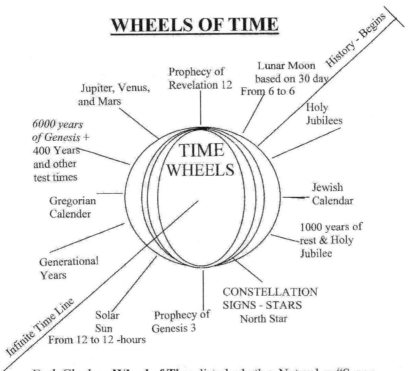

Each Clock or **Wheel of Time** listed whether Natural or "Supernatural" has a beginning and an end, and they converge with one another to form foot prints in history that we can learn from. God has appointed a special group of Time Wheels to measure and mark special events, Divine Prophecy, and the end of the Age!. Only the Time Line is infinite, with History having a beginning!.

The illustration on figure 6 shows some of the various "*Wheels of Time*" - most are natural Time Wheels related to the moon and sun, but some relate to the very ordered Jubilee and Shemitah years. Some are related to the larger countdown in years such as 1000-year period or the testimonies of Prophets such as Daniel and Zechariah. The "*Garden of Eden to Infinity timeline,*" goes through the various Wheels of Time, and a supernatural time wheel we cannot fathom, for it determines the Lord's return. The *Wheels of Time chart* links generational periods to the entire timeline of life. This timeline is eternal and thus supernatural in that we do not know its end time. It goes through the center of each time-wheel discussed. Not shown on this timeline is the 10-year period the Lord gives through the Sign of Revelation 12.

The Sign in the sun, moon, and stars form one Wheel and the Jewish Feast days along with the blood moons and the conjunction of Venus and Jupiter form another Wheel of time. The earlier wheel of time convergence chart in Figure 3 shows a convergence of prophetic time spans related to the Feast Days and blood moons and goes clockwise like a watch to show that time is running out like a stopwatch. It is a countdown. Putting all this into perspective we can see a sequence of dates and numbers on a timeline showing God's footprint in history. As will be shown in Chapters 5 - 6 there is much more to the Wheels of Time than meets the eye. They do intersect with God's timeline here on earth and they also connect with the supernatural realm. We are eternally connected to the supernatural. The question that each of us must answer is: *"Can I believe and trust in a God who loves me so much that He would leave the expanse of heaven to become like me and die for me as an eternal sacrifice for my sins? Will you make this choice soon or will you let Time make the decision for you?"*

In 2017 the Jewish New Year began on September 22$^{nd}$ and the Sign on the 23$^{rd}$. The new year was 5778. In 10 years, the new year will be 5788 or a year of "double trouble" or "double Beginnings." This could be the year of the Abomination of Desolation. Let's therefore discuss the special meaning of the Jewish number 8. Eight people were in the Ark to begin a new world, and 8 days of lamp oil changed the heart of the Jews seeking a sign from God and a new beginning for their faith during the heavy persecution by the Seleucid Empire. Eight was the age of a baby's circumcision. Eight to most Jews represents a step into a new stage of life or a new beginning. This new double 88 will be very ominous as the New Beginnings could involve Satan's visitation.

The year 2017 was a special year for both America and Israel. Note that September 23 was the first full day into the New Year of 5778, and a transition to new beginnings. Based on our calendar system we would call this the beginning of the year 2017-18. Throughout history it seems as if this 17-18 combination carries importance. Is it because the number 1 is the number for God and 7 is for perfection with as 8 means new beginnings? We shall see if there is more to these Wheels of Time than already explained. Ezekiel's Wheels in Heaven are active and represent more than a physical ball of vitreous tissue.

If the Sign of September 23rd is true, then the Cosmic Event in figure 7 on the next page could correlate to other signposts in history that may reflect God's Timing for fulfilling His promises and prophecy. For instance, is there a significant pattern in what happened in each of 40 Jubilee years going back from Sept 23, 2017. Counting back 40 Jubilees or 2000 years we arrive at 17-18 AD. Jesus was born in 2-3 BC and many believe that twenty was the age of accountability or the age of transition to manhood. Twenty was the normal time for military induction and the age required to pay tithes. In the Hebraic culture it is a number for completion and sufficiency. So, if we add 20 years to the timeline of Jesus Christ, the calendar reads 17-18 AD, which many believe was the first Jubilee year of the Messianic age.

Check out the unique diagram on the next page Figure 7. This shows how the birth of the nation of Israel in 48 compares to the Birth of Jesus Christ in 3 BC. The ancient Essene calendar which is a solar and lunar calendar shows that from the Creation to the flood there were 1948 days. God's timing is perfect, and time past seems to carry a prophetic message forward to the future. The Essenes had the most accurate calendar of ancient days with a 364-day year and through the study of Daniel they were able to predict the accurate arrival of the Messiah. Many believe they knew Jesus was the Messiah and that they were in contact with both John the Baptist and Jesus. According to their calendar Jesus was crucified in 32 AD. His 2nd Coming would measure exactly 2000 years later in 2032 AD. That would make the year 2024-25 of particular importance when you add 7 years for the Tribulation period on Daniel's 70th week.

The next Jubilee was 67-68 AD, the time of Nero's persecution and the execution of both Peter and Paul. What is also interesting is how the combination of 20 + 50, creates two powerful prophetic 70- year periods in both centuries. Ours started in 1947-48 with the birth of the nation of Israel and ended on Sept. 20-22, 2017. After 67 AD a 10-year diaspora scattered the Jews all over the world. For more information on the birth of Jesus Christ check out the latest version of the Cosmic Crossroad Countdown series called: The Invisible War & Final Chapter.

## The Prophetic Jubilee & Birth Timeline

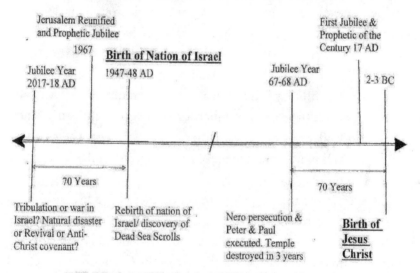

Jerusalem Reunified and Prophetic Jubilee
1967
Jubilee Year 2017-18 AD

Birth of Nation of Israel
1947-48 AD

First Jubilee & Prophetic of the Century 17 AD

Jubilee Year 67-68 AD

2-3 BC

70 Years

70 Years

Tribulation or war in Israel? Natural disaster or Revival or Anti-Christ covenant?

Rebirth of nation of Israel/ discovery of Dead Sea Scrolls

Nero persecution & Peter & Paul executed. Temple destroyed in 3 years

Birth of Jesus Christ

Within 2 Prophetic Jubilee Periods are the Birth of Jesus Christ and Israel!
Timeline Spans 2000 years from 17 AD to now or 40 Jubilees - Bracketed by Two 70 year periods

**Figure 7**

As we saw earlier the birth of Jesus started a whole new era but was 2-3 years earlier than the Gregorian calendar records. This earlier birth matches up with Herod the Great's death. When we adjust for those 3 years and add them to 17, it totals 20 years. Adding the 20 to the 50- year Jubilee gets us up to 67-68 AD which would be the end of the 1st Prophetic 70-year generation period in the era of the New

Covenant. If we accept 1947-48 as the prophetic birth or budding of Israel, we can conclude that we are in another 70-year Prophetic generation of the New Covenant. Will the Cosmic Crossroad that we are experiencing lead to a prophetic covenant with Israel by 2024-25? If so this could be a time when the Anti-Christ will make his appearance.

Figure 7 shows that the year 67-68 AD was a dark time for the early church for it was the year when both the Apostles Peter and Paul were executed by the Emperor Nero. Now if we go to our present century and add 50 years to the rebirth of Israel in 1947-48, we arrive at 1997-98 which also was a dark year. This was the year when the last settlement in Gaza was forced to surrender to the Hamas Palestinian coalition. Both 1997 and 67AD were dark years in the eyes of God; and we can include 1967. They belong in the two 70-year periods that bracket the 20 centuries. These two prophetic 70-year periods incorporate: 1) A prophetic Jubilee year, 2) A miraculous birth, 3) Followed by a dark year affecting God's people. As stated earlier we are in God's timeline of history, and we seem to be at a remarkably interesting Cosmic Crossroad in his Plan for our last generation.

Check the two 20-year post-birth periods and how they match. The 1947-48 to the 6-Day War of 1967 was a maturing time for the new nation. Following the timeline, we see that the maturation of Jesus Christ into manhood spanned 2-3 BC to 17- 18 AD. The 1967 war was another miracle war much like their war in 1947; in each case Israel defeated armies ten times their size and strength. Now add a 50-year Jubilee to both and we see great changes in the paradigm for America and for Israel. Israel blossomed with wealth and prosperity and so did America. The church also blossomed whereas Israel has become mired in orthodoxy and secularism. What is next?

Another correlation to consider is that 17-18 AD + 2000 years = 2017-18. Two thousand years is 40 X 50 years, or 40 Jubilees.

We have already seen that a Jubilee period is very significant to God. In the Bible, the 40-year period is considered a *complete time of purification and testing.* We can conclude that 2000 years is the ultimate test of mankind's spiritual pulse and wellbeing? Is God using this time to measure the hearts and minds of people before completing His plan? Have we passed the test and are we now ready for the next phase or paradigm? We saw what happened in the approximate 1500 years of life before and during Noah's time. God had to cut short His plan and use the worldwide flood to destroy the first creation on earth because of sin. Is the church ready for the rapture?

Adam's sin against God and against God's best intent for mankind and for creation caused a major detour. A similar type of situation happened to the nation of Israel before they were able to settle the promised land. Like Adam and Eve and all those who heard God's message of love and mercy, these Israelites knew God was a God of miracles and compassion. For over a year they had witnessed His miraculous provision of food, clothing, shoes, water, and the Law. His mercies were new every morning as He guided and protected this nation of men, women, and children with a pillar of fire and a pillar of smoke. As before, the number 40 ended up playing a key role in the test of that Hebrew generation so that His Plan could and would be fulfilled.

The big test happened at Kadesh Barnea to God's chosen people, the Israelites, as they received a view of the Promised Land. They sent spies into the land that reported abundant resources, but then advised not to advance and move forward because there were too many *giants in the land.* Because this first generation of Israelites let fear dictate their hearts, God had that generation spend 40 years wandering in the wilderness; until finally their generation died off. The 40 days that the 10 spies embraced fear instead of a trust in God would determine the length of time of punishment. Out of that entire generation only Caleb and Joshua showed faith in the face of enemy giants. God therefore allowed only those two from that generation to enter the Promised Land. And God will allow only those who have faith in Him to enter His Kingdom. God takes obedience and trust very seriously.

About 1,500 years later Israel again made a bad decision and rejected God's Provision and Promise of Redemption. They rejected the Kingdom of God and sacrificed their Messiah. Two thousand years before the birth of Jesus Christ, God had made a covenant with Abraham. *"I will make of you a great nation, and I will bless you, and make your name great; and you shall be a blessing. And I will bless them that bless you and curse him that curses you: and in you shall all families of the earth be blessed,"* Gen. 12:1-3. This Covenant promised that all descendants would be blessed, and Isaac and Jacob were *"heirs with him of the same promise."* From his descendants would come the One who would Redeem us all, Jesus Christ. The birth of Jesus stands in the center of two 2000-year periods that branch out from the birth of Jesus like the arms of a cross.

Jesus Christ is the center of History, the fulfillment of Genesis 3:15, the Answer to Adam's Fall, the Incarnation and fulfillment of the Abrahamic Covenant, the Promise and Purpose of all Prophecy, and the power of the Cross and Resurrection that reconciled all mankind to God. God introduced a completely new paradigm that transformed the measurement of eternity in the hearts of man. God's space, time, and mass were all subject to this reconciliation. He put eternity in our hearts, and His Book of Life in heaven records steps in our divine transformation. Reference figure 5 A & B and check out the graph.

2 Corinthians 3:14, states, *"But their minds were hardened. For to this day, when they read the old covenant, that same veil remains uplifted, because only through Christ is it taken away. Yes, to this day whenever Moses is read a veil lies over their hearts. But when one turns to the Lord, the veil is removed."* Let us help God defeat hardened minds and veiled hearts!

Does 40 X 50 or 2000-years mean a complete testing of the earth and its nations in preparation for His Return and Judgment? There may be more truth hidden in this timeline than we care to admit. It is no coincidence that God picked the man Abraham, to anchor all the nations of the world to the seed mentioned in Genesis 3:15 with it all happening in 2 periods of 2000 years. The Jubilee was a time for mercy and release, so could there be a 2000 year span of Mercy and New Beginnings necessary before justice is reconciled through Jesus Christ? His first Coming reconciled the world to God and His second will bring Judgment and the Fullness of His Kingdom.

His Second coming will be a surprise like the Noah's flood was, as all life will be judged; with everyone and everything on earth experiencing God's judgment. Jesus Christ is the 2nd Adam, who will restore what was lost due to Adam's sin. Jesus Christ will deliver the righteous remnant on a spiritual ark to a New Beginning in time and life. This divine ark will carry the saved through the space-time continuum into an eternal relationship with God. We will see how 2, 5, 10, 20, 40, 50, 70, 100, 400, 500 and 2000 year-spans play a role in the convergence of God's Cosmic Wheels of Time. Pray about this and let the Holy Spirit inspire you, as these numbers converge to answer prophecy and fulfill a Jubilee pattern of return and release. The Word suggests that God will fulfill prophecy when the numbers are complete. (Reference the Fig. 6). The Wheels of time will help everyone to see how God may be syncing time in many dimensions. These wheels of course do not include the most important dimension and that is the eternal one which has no wheel because it is eternal and may just flow through and around these other wheels like a spiral. This eternal timeline is where these number combinations and generations converge to show us footprints that help us determine the course of history. The Wheels of Time and the Wheels of Omniscience will be covered Chapters 5 and 6.

*"Through his power all things were made things in heaven and on earth, seen and not seen - all spiritual rulers, lords, powers, and authorities. Everything was made through him and for him. The Son was there before anything was made. And all things continue because of him,"* Col.1:16-17.

We can easily see that God generated order in all the forms of Creation, from the smallest snail or leaf to the largest spiral galaxy. He uses number combinations, math, and mathematical sequences to reveal Truth and beauty to us in incredible ways. We see this amazing order in the Fibonacci ratio - which is a universal mathematical sequence illustrating order in both form and structure of living and non- living entities, from spiral galaxies to the breaking of waves, to snails. The ratio from one spiral layer to the next in a snail, or from one floret level to another on flowers, or one vein pattern to the next on a leaf, or one bract pattern to the next on a pinecone, and likewise for the pineapple is a specific ratio related to the Fibonacci sequence. Fractals and their simple formulas have sequences that spread into infinity and are examples of how God has ordered all of creation to follow simple mathematical formulas that define their shape, function, and form. God in his infinite wisdom created science and math so that we could appreciate his order and Glory. He set the world in motion, and He therefore set the clocks and created time. The Wheels of Time and Jubilees are ordered along God's eternal timeline and where they intersect is what this book calls a "*Crossroad.*"

"*He defeated the rulers and powers of the spiritual world. With the cross, he won the victory over them and led them away, as defeated, and powerless prisoners for the whole world to see,*" Colossians 2:15.

We seem to be at an especially important "*Cosmic Crossroa*d" that links God's time to man's time and joining Judaic prophetic signs to Gentile Signs of the End Time. This is all part of His order and plan. Just as God used the stars to point to His first coming, does it not make sense that He will again use the stars and constellations to point to His second Coming? Twelve is the number of Perfection and Authority, but also of "TIME" set by God in the natural world of the moon, sun, stars, and constellations, (12 months, 12 Constellation Signs, and two sets of 12 hours). Twelve is also an interesting number combination of the perfect unit 2 found in all of creation and the number 10 of purification.

The number two defines a dynamic coexistence of opposites or contrasts that balance forces, entities, divinity, space, and matter. All of creation is a balance of 2's. Two can be looked at as a unit such as male and female, or the *Hypostatic Union of God* and man, or light and darkness. God in fact designed His Creation to witness both Good and Evil. Thus, the number 12 could be looked at as a universal number for order in God's Divine Plan for creation in both space and time! Twelve measures local time not heavenly time.

By studying His Creation in the Light of His Word we can see the natural and the supernatural converging on these significant signposts. Revelation 12 takes us back in time to His original warning in Gen. 3:15. It is a *"Spiritual Time Wheel"* that connects to our physical time wheels. It does have a beginning and an end because Satan is crushed and defeated, but its consequences are eternal. God spoke to the Serpent and told him that his head would be crushed by the *"Seed of the Woman."* This coming judgment will eventually bring all creation back to perfection under the authority of the *"Seed of Adam,"* Jesus Christ. The saving of a remnant that started in the flood has continued with the nation of Israel and continues to this day.

Right now, the promise that Jesus made in Matthew 16:18 is being fulfilled as He builds his Church, and the gates of Hades cannot prevail. The Great Sign, a signpost marking it in our time. Genesis 3:15 and Revelation 12 align the Promises made by God in the Garden of Eden 6000 years ago with the Promise to the Church today. Those promises point to the defeat of Satan, or dragon, and his evil intentions. Daniel's prophecy of 70 weeks ties the last *week* or 7 years to God's divine Crossroad where stars, Jubilee years, and the prophetic generation meet on the historical timeline.

Jesus said, *"I am the Door. If anyone enters by Me, he will come in and go out and find pasture. A thief (Satan) comes to kill, to steal, and to destroy,"* John 10:9-10.

As we saw in Chapter 3, Revelation 12 has 12 bright stars in the Constellation Leo to adorn the head of Virgo. Leo is also the 12th Sign in the Heavens. Twelve comes into play at the center of our Cosmic stage. Twelve is an important number in Revelation as it applies to the 24 elders: 12 + 12 seated before the throne in Revelation 4. The heavenly city has 12 foundations and 12 gates, and its dimension is 12000 by 12000 by 12000. The number of those sealed is 12,000 X 12,000 = 144,000. God's Cosmic Clock starts with a 12-hour day and a 12-hour night, then a 12-month yearly calendar, and an array of 12 constellation signs forming their own wheel of time and space in the heavenly realm. Reference Fig 6 and check the other Wheels that orient supernatural time to natural time.

Most of our Signs are arranged in a circle like a clock. We remember that 7 is the perfect number and so when you add 5 it becomes the number 12 which often completes a perfect sequence or natural order for time and execution. The number 5 is a number for God's Grace since Jesus took 5 loaves and David used 5 stones. Added again to 12, it equals 17 the key date for the Jubilee year that begins each century. Or two 5's equal 10 which is the Holy number we talked about much earlier. Also note that 1,200 years times 5 (for Grace) equals 6000 years! We are approaching the end of this important mark in time. Each of these steps in time point to a divine crossroad countdown in God's sequenced *"Wheels of Time."* Each wheel of time intersects with God's timeline. The special dates that link up and act as markers on the timeline will mark periods like the Jubilee years where the *"lost time"* is recorded but not counted. Our timeline has a beginning, but no end. It is eternal and thus is supernatural and under the control of God.

So far, you have seen a lot of numbers and a lot of sequences, and dates. Since 6 is the number for man, 6000 years represents a completion of Life and God's Grace + Mercy dispensed on earth for mankind There is a pattern and a purpose to this including His creation. His footprints run the course of history and point to a convergence of events that will happen soon. These events are laid out in Daniel's prophecy of the last week, or 7 years. Just as God has named the stars, He also given purpose to years, dates, and numbers.

Everything He has done, is doing, and will do has order and a purpose. God wants us to understand what is going on in around us, so that we do not panic when trials begin! As you contemplate what this may mean to you, pray, and read the four Gospels in the Bible. So, confess that Jesus is Lord and believe that He rose from the dead, then He will save you.

In the Rabbinic calendar, this year is designated the year 5777. The "777," is particularly important to the Jewish mind because it symbolizes total or perfect completion on His eternal timeline! And as we stated earlier the #5 is important to us because it is a sign of Grace: for example in Revelation Chapter 6 in the midst of a series of "seal judgments," there is the 5th seal from which we see an appeal at the altar by the blood of Christian martyrs for vengeance! But God says to wait until the time is fulfilled.

The Balfour agreement happened in 1917, ending the 400-year Ottoman Empire's control of Jerusalem! The Gentile component related to this date was the League of Nation's Mandate that put Jerusalem under the control of the British who were the largest Christian Empire in the world. In that time span the British expanded the Christian mission throughout India and the world. As was shown earlier the nation of Israel was formed almost the same time as the Dead Sea Scrolls were discovered in 1947-48. That discovery completely changed the landscape in academic circles. Here for the first time was proof that the Bible was transcribed perfectly from generation to generation and that the context was completely accurate. It proved that the book of Daniel is Prophetic since it was written hundreds of years earlier. Therefore, the discovery was one of the greatest events to happen in the Christian arena in the 20th century and will be discussed further in the Chapter on testimonies.

Also going back 500 years, in the year 1517, Luther nailed the 95 Thesis at Wittenberg. On the Jewish side, in the year 1517, we saw that the Ottoman Empire took over all of Palestine and Egypt. This "Assyrian-like" aggressor held Jerusalem for 400 years. As stated earlier most of these divine dates have both a Jewish and a Gentile component. The numbers 40 and 400 illustrate how a time of *"personal and national testing"* can be connected to a Gentile period of testing. The Ottoman's control of Jerusalem put them under God's Judgment! Check Figure 3.

Taking God's land away from Israel is a serious venture that will bring God's eventual judgment, just as it did for the Babylonians and the Persians. The number 400 is 10 X 40 or an extended testing to the point of national purification or release of land back to God. It makes sense that in these *"Generational Periods"* the land was taken over by "enemy" nations that controlled the land for a set time. Out of the old Ottoman Empire emerged an emancipated Turkey with a secular government respecting other religions. They did develop a good relationship with Israel after and during the 9th Jubilee. This 400-year time span might be considered a Return of the Holy land to Israel.

The Holy land was not connected to any Israelite tribe before or after 1947-48. So, would Jubilee periods be linked to the land of Israel then and now? Probably not. This would not be true of Jerusalem. Jerusalem is God's Holy city where Mount Moriah stands and where Abraham made his sacrifice of faith to the LORD. *"On the mountain of the LORD it will be provided,"* Genesis 22:14. Note, the transition of 20 years puts us at 1967- 68 which was the birth of the reunified Jerusalem.

Remember that we have established 20 years as the age for the transition from child to adult and from child to a divine accountability (this was the age for making the first tithe and serving in the military). Another important twenty-year period began with 3 BC (the actual birth of Jesus Christ) and ended with Him being 20 years of age in the AD era of 17 AD which would have been the first Jubilee in the modern era. So, here we see the birth of reunified Jerusalem in 1967 is a parallel to the birth of the Savior, 1950 years later. Fifty years after that we are in 2017 and the Sign of the Woman. Refer to figure 7 to see the remarkable parallels to the birth of both.

About 1000 years after Abraham made an altar at this very location, King David bought the threshing floor from *Arunah the Jebusite* and built his altar to the Lord, so that a *"plague may be held back from the people"* (2 Samuel 24:18, 21). Could this have been a Jubilee year? Why had David been so determined to go against the advice of others and take a census unless it was an incredibly special time? After David's death, his son King Solomon built one of the *"Seven Wonders of the World,"* the First Temple on the same site. Solomon's temple lasted for about four hundred years, until it was destroyed by Babylonian armies in 587-6 BC. Note 400 is the complete time of testing before deliverance.

The city of Jerusalem, I believe, is one of the keys to Prophecy for this will be His throne from which He will rule. That is why I have included the *"Testimony of God's Holy City, Jerusalem,"* in Chapter 6. Amazingly, if you add the years from the birth of Adam to the point of God's "seed" covenant with Abraham it equals 1948 years which is the exact time in our Gregorian calendar that the nation of Israel was born. This is another perplexing wheel of time.

This twenty-year transition added to a 50-year Jubilee equals the 70-year last generation that we discussed earlier. This prophetic generational period started in 1947-48, as shown in the fig. 7 graph. All of this reveals a harmony in history that testifies to how carefully God orchestrates His Plan for Israel and for the world throughout time. This is a testimony of God's Love for His People even after the "Great Diaspora" and the "Holocaust." The land that God gave the Israelites was Holy land and therefore a price had to be paid. The land was laid to waste just as Isaiah said it would; remember our discussion on the Fig tree and on Isaiah's lesson in Chapter 5:5-6. Countless wars have been fought over this land and a lot of blood was spilled. So, what will happen next? Will Israel go through a major test, maybe a war with Iran, where a hero will step in and save the day? He will then make a covenant with Israel *"for a lasting peace"* and the Temple will be built over the destruction of the Dome of the Rock.

Zechariah 12:10, *"And I will pour upon the house of David, and upon the inhabitants of Jerusalem, the spirit of grace and of supplications: and they shall look upon me whom they have pierced, and they shall mourn for him."*

The following verses help to illustrates part of the dynamic connection of the line of David and the throne of God. This was a blood or "spiritual connection" through Jesus Christ, who was born of a virgin. *"Therefore, since we are surrounded by so great a cloud of witnesses, let us also lay aside every weight, and sin which clings so closely, and let us run with endurance the race that is set before looking to Jesus, the founder and perfecter of our faith, who for the joy that was set before him endured the cross, despising the shame, and is seated at the right hand of the throne of God."* Heb. 12:1-2. Jesus our champion and the root of David, will defeat the enemy serpent as promised by God in Genesis 3:15.

Concerning our own limited knowledge and bias, Solomon wrote: *"Trust in the LORD with all your heart, and do not depend on your own understanding. In all your ways acknowledge him, and he will make your paths straight. Do not be wise in your own eyes; fear the LORD and turn away from evil. This will bring healing to your body, and refreshment to your bones,"* Prov. 3:5-8.

Understanding this simple verse, created a fire that changed my life! This is when God showed me how wrong evolution is and when He opened the Word of God to my heart for the first time. No longer was it my brain that was dictating my thoughts and my behavior, but it was the New Heart that he gave me that took over. So, be humble and seek to open new doors - *"If you seek me, you will find me!"*

Too many leaders today are not concerned by "numbers and dates" and have a closed mind concerning prophetic Signs such as God's Great Sign of Revelation 12. They may have been discouraged by their teachers who told them that prophecy was not important. These teachers are misleading people for the Word of God has over 25% of its content dedicated to warning and educating the reader about the future. Over three hundred were fulfilled exactly as promised when Jesus Christ completed His first Coming. These prophetic promises are a Testimony to the accuracy and power of the Word of God. Those who ignore them will be held accountable for disparaging the Word and those who are trying to warn the lost.

This book is a *"Caution Sign"* warning everyone to pray, seek God, and read the Bible with an open heart and mind. Do not depend on the traditions of man and empty philosophy as the Apostle Paul states. Agendas, money, pride, and debt will distract the church and its leaders. As people who are privileged to have a choice, we should follow what God is putting in our hearts and mind. It is a real privilege to pray and to have a road map and life manual called the Bible to read and study. The Bible is the Word of God, and it is *"living and active,"* just as we are living stones, and in heaven the living creatures have the Omniscient *"wheels of eyes."* Do they see into our hearts, as God works to transform His creation?

*"For the word of God is living and active, sharper than any two-edged sword, piercing to the division of soul and of spirit, of joints and of marrow, and discerning the thoughts and intentions of the heart. And no creature is hidden from his sight, but all are naked and exposed to the eyes of him to whom we must give account."* (Hebrews 4:12-13). I will discuss this more in Chapter 5 and 6. The answer to what is the Wheels of Time is summarized there. However, you might gain some understanding from what was just said in this paragraph. There is a divine light shining in our worldly wilderness and that Light is the Power of the Cross. We must share it quickly, for we do not have the time that the Lost Generation had 3500 years ago. America is not Israel and it will not be preserved by God to fulfill any prophecy. The remnant promised are those who place their Trust in the Saving Power of the Blood of Christ.

Peter the Apostle warns us to, *"Rid yourselves of all wickedness, deceit, hypocrisy, envy, and slander."* And he continues, *"the stone that the builders rejected - this One has become the cornerstone."* And then he warns, *"I urge you as aliens and temporary residents to abstain from fleshy desires that war against you."* Then after much sharing concludes,

*"Be sober! Be on the alert! Your adversary the Devil is prowling around like a roaring lion, looking for anyone he can devour. Resist him, firm in the faith, knowing that the same sufferings are being experienced by your brothers in the world."* I Peter 2:1-5:9.

Slander is much worse than people realize for it results in damage to all involved. Those who listen to slander need to beware for not only can it hurt you, but if you pass it on, you will be just as guilty. Slander relates to what was said earlier about reconciliation and remorse during the 10 Days of Awe. By tradition, the Jews thought that God was keeping a set of books on everyone and would judge them accordingly. This is supported by what Jesus Christ said, *"But I tell you that every careless word that people speak, they shall give an accounting for it in the day of judgment,"* Matt. 12:36.

We all remember as children what happened to Samson, who squandered God's blessings to feed his desire. He lost the very eyes that had led him to sin. Our country cannot afford to be led away by lust and greed and the resulting perversion and loss of innocence. One result of this run-away lust is the high abortion rate and a resulting mental and spiritual illness in our nation.

The "dragon" is real and so is prophecy! Most people cannot pick up a Bible and read it with understanding, because of its power. It is the Living Word. But if you seek the truth with humility and an open heart, *"He may exalt you in due time,"* for *"God resists the proud, but gives Grace to the humble,"* 1 Peter 5:5-6. Then Peter gives an answer, *"Cast all your cares upon Him, because he cares for you."* God works in us and for us even at the worst of times. He wants us to depend on Him and to pray for the Lord's return to hasten His coming! Peter continues, *"For we did not follow cleverly contrived myths when we made known to you the power and coming of our Lord Jesus Christ."* And concludes, *"No prophecy of Scripture comes from one's own interpretation, because no prophecy ever came by the will of man; instead, moved by the Holy Spirit, men spoke from God."* As you can see, we have transitioned into what I call the *Testimony of Peter.*

Peter warns, *"First be aware of this: scoffers will come in the last days to scoff, following their own lusts, saying, 'Where is the promise of His coming? – long ago the heavens and the earth were formed out of water and through water by the Word of God. But by the same Word the present heavens and earth are held in store for fire,"* 2 Peter 1:4 and 3:9. This is God's science.

These "scoffers" are back. Peter warns: *"The Day of the Lord will come like a thief—therefore, since you have been forewarned, be on your guard, so that you are not led away by the error of the immoral and fall,"* 2 Peter 3:10-17.

Peter knows how Jesus cared for him when he made mistakes and failed. Jesus was always there to encourage him and lift him back up. Likewise, he knows that even when tribulation comes the Lord will be there with us. We can know that when the seven years of Daniel's final *week* comes, God will be there to protect His Church. We will be getting to the dynamics of this *70-weeks Prophecy* soon.

Just know that "scoffers" who are living it up in the world or have their own agendas, will say: *"Hey, since it did not happen the last time, they said judgment was coming, it will never happen, let's have some fun."* But Peter reminds us that many were saying foolish things before the flood destroyed everything. Peter concludes with a chilling statement: *"The Day of the Lord"* or the wrath of God *"will come like a thief."* Few people discuss this since most Prophecy scholars believe that the church will already be raptured. However, the vast majority who do not make the rapture should prepare for this tragic *"Day of the Lord"* which will come quickly just as the rapture will come in *"the twinkling of an eye"* Maranatha - the Lord comes.

Peter's generation saw the first coming of the Lord and witnessed intense persecution. In comparison, we have witnessed evil empires and defeated them, and in this country, we have not seen persecution in America. Are we *"on guard,"* as Peter states, or are we allowing the enemy in? The result of our recent election shows the deep divide within ethnic groups and age levels in our society. The fabric appears torn by hatred, lust, and a rebellious anger. Some are raising the flag and others are stomping on it. Some are lifting hands to God and others are angry with a tirade of anti-authority demands and behavior.

The traditional fabric is being trampled on and set on fire! Yet, God is with us, and our country continues to seek the high ground. We can learn from history, from other generations, and from the words of God, or we can go our own way and lose our way. That is one reason why we need to continue to look at Prophecy and realize that this confusion may be God's plan.

In the process of purging apathy and shaking society God wants the Church to seize the opportunity to rescue the lost with the Gospel before the storm grows. We can see how past generations failed to act as darkness grew. Major enemies surprised European society in the 16th century. In 1517 the Ottoman Empire scourged much of Europe and took over Palestine and Egypt. They held onto Jerusalem until 1917 which is exactly 400 years.

Looking back from 2017 we see this as a prophetic 500-year period. God seems to have been in control of this cloud of destruction and fear that swept towards Europe for so long. In and around 1917 the Turks committed genocide against the state of Armenia, which to this day they refuse to admit responsibility for! After they were defeated a stable secular nation of Turkey rose out of the ashes.

Now 100 years later Turkey is no longer a modern secular state since dictator Erdogan canceled the constitution and removed the office of Prime Minister. He has sacked and arrested many people in higher office including judges and all opposition leaders. He has taken control of the media and is removing vestiges of Christianity. Recently he attacked our allies the Kurds (many who are Christians). He has been in power for over 33 years and has claimed that he is a Caliph.

He may soon try to claim a "United State of Islam" and threaten the sovereignty of the Kurds. He like the leaders of Iran could foment a war in the Middle East to gain power. Take careful note that the 400 and 500-year spans mentioned above are God-prints in that

Jubilee Clock. Each fall on Jubilee years and so does the important 100-year period. Note how 100-year periods are marked with war and a purging of land and humanity.

We know that mullahs in Iran and want to start an *"Apocalyptic War"* to usher in the Grand Mahdi who they believe will save Islam and defeat the infidels. One popular Sheik says, *"He is coming, but his arrival will be after the great war. It will be the fight of the big powers with each other... after that a savior will come."* Many Islamists and other militant fundamentalists believe that since America has gone to bed with the devil, we consort to spread wickedness and vile thinking, making us, the "anti-Christ." Their "savior," the Mahdi will become the 12th Imam, who is then joined by their version of Jesus Christ. Their version of Jesus may be the anti-Christ who will then authenticate the Mahdi's title.

From the Christian perspective, this Grand Mahdi might gain power after a war much like the Gog and Magog war in Ezekiel 38-39 or a kind of "neighbors war." Their savior or the anti-Christ will then make a false covenant with the nation of Israel. He will then break the covenant when he commits the "Abomination of Desolation" and declares himself to be God. From the Christian perspective Jesus Christ, comes to the rescue after 7 years of tribulation and defeats the Anti-Christ (possibly the grand Mahdi) at the war of Armageddon. Islamists will expect their prophet Jesus to affirm the Grand Mahdi, but instead Jesus Christ will destroy him and all his forces.

Considering what was stated in the previous paragraph, some believe that the traditional theologians are mistaken in thinking that the Anti-Christ will come out of the European Common Market to claim a Roman or Vatican throne. They believe that it will instead be a Caliphate of 10 crowns. Joel Richardson the author of the Mid-East Beast believes that we have overlooked some of the crucial facts. He points out that the Roman Empire was never the *"Beast with iron teeth"* since it issued the "Pax Romana" and built all the infrastructure that made possible the fulfillment of Prophecy in the time of Jesus. He contends that the Islamic Caliphate and other groups related to

Islam were the ones who decimated the entire region with Jerusalem at the center. And that it would better fit Daniel's vision of the Iron Beast *"that crushed and devoured its victims and trampled underneath whatever was left,"* Dan.7:7. This iron toothed beast, however, must have a very sophisticated military, and therefore it makes more sense that it has a European connection rooted in the ancient Holy Roman Empire. We may soon see how the 10 horns play out.

The main support for a Rome centered "Beast" is the statement mentioning the *"City of 7 hills,"* fitting Rome or even "New York" which at one time had 7 hills. The actual sequence of Empires from Babylon to the Roman Empire also supports this popular view. However, the two legs of the *"Great Image"* that Nebuchadnezzar saw in his famous dream, which Daniel interpreted in Daniel 2, best represents the split in the Islamic movement than it does the two Roman periods of time. The Great Image's legs are equal in size and length like the Sunni and Shiite sects which grew together in history. Unlike the Islamic sects the Roman periods existed at different times, had different capitals, and were much different in size and length of domination. So, this is a plus for Joel. However, I still favor the New Roman Empire concept. We have seen growing power and weaknesses in the leadership of the Roman Catholic Church in each passing generation and a movement towards a one-world religious system.

Let us review historical Biblical Generations. From all the calculations, we have 3 Major Generational periods pointing to an end generation in 2017-18, and 4 minor ones. Here is recap of the top 3 major Biblical generations and the 3 dates that fulfill prophecy for the nation of Israel: Using the birth-day of the nation of Israel in 1947-48, the recapture of Jerusalem in 1967, and the issuing of the Balfour Declaration in 1917, we notice that the "50" for Jubilee equals "Release or Return," the "70" equals "Prophecy Complete," and the 100 equals *"Time Extended"* for testing. All point to a period after 2017-18 when God will introduce a new paradigm and the invisible war begins.

Behind these generational periods are the other supporting periods such as the 400, 500 and even the 1000-year Jubilee periods. We will see how the 40-year generation period spiritually intersects with multiple 400-year periods and other extended times of purification. God penalized the nation of Israel a total of 40 years, or one year for each day that the spies lacked faith in their 40-day period spying out of the "enemy" land. This was a unique period for Israel. We will soon see in Chapter 6, how this time of purification also links to the *"Cross in the Wilderness"* to us. Will God put the Church through a period of purification throughout a wilderness type trial until 2024-25.

Only two of the twelve spies that entered the land came back with a hopeful outlook. These two men, Caleb, and Joshua placed their trust in God's ability to lead them and defeat the giants in the land. One of those giants, Goliath, made history a generation later when he challenged David and was taken down by a rock guided by God's hand. Throughout history God has raised up people with faith to defeat enemies and overcome fear and doubt. He raises and protects a righteous remnant to carry the banner of redemption. Because the report from most of the spies was man-centered and fear based despite all that God had communicated and done for them, God would judge their rejection and would give them what they wanted. He gave them the safety of the wilderness for 40 years.

Likewise, in our modern wilderness there are many who do not want a relationship with God and God will give them the eternal separation that they desire. The generation of Israelites would live out their own fear, wandering with their families until they died in the wilderness. They were therefore called *"the Lost Generation,"* *which is a fitting title for the lost who seek their own way, and de*sire to be captains of their own soul. This is a picture of what happens when God offers the free Gift of Salvation, yet one chooses to reject Him. He gives you what you want. You will get eternal separation from Him which is another word for Hell. If you place your trust in God, He will lead you out of your wandering and will bring you into the promised land of Heaven and a life in fellowship with the God that created the Universe.

Considering all that I have said above, a 400-year period would be an extended period of judgment and evaluation. God gave the Jews an extended 400 years of slavery and later of silent testing before the birth of the Savior. He also gave them 400 years to be led and encouraged by the Judges and almost 400 years to enjoy Solomon's Temple. He made generations wait for His deliverance. Think of how many Jews died in Goshen, Egypt, and did not get to see God's deliverance through Joshua and Moses. But imagine how many more did not have the privilege of seeing the Savior come or meet Him. A period of 400 years is a long time to wait and believe. We have waited about 2000 years or 5 of these four-hundred-year periods for the Lord's Return! Is America ready? Polls show that only 9% of Americans open a Bible.

When we consider the length of a generation most people do not think 40 years is accurate. In the case of the "Lost Generation," Caleb and Joshua were young grown men when the generation began but there were many much older. The average age would certainly not be less than 25-35 years which when added to the 40, it would make the wilderness generation age to be about 70. The average time between 100 years and 40 years is also 70 years, which would make more sense for a true physical generation. With our extended lifespan it makes sense that the generation of grace would now equal 80 years.

Seventy years is also considered the time of a Prophetic Generation as spoken by the prophet Daniel. Amazingly, the Shemitah cycle is connected to Daniel's 70-week prophecy, which ends in a seven-year Tribulation period. From Daniel 9:24, Daniel is visited by Gabriel God's messenger who encourages him by explaining the future: *"God has allowed 70 weeks for your people and your holy city, Daniel. The 70 weeks are ordered for these reasons: to stop doing bad things, to stop sinning, to make people pure, to bring the goodness that continues forever, to put a seal on visions and prophets, and to dedicate a very holy place."* Daniel who studied the Stars and left his writings to the Magi gives us a supernatural vision into the future. This vision has not yet been completely fulfilled. I will show you why.

Most scholars interpret the angel Gabriel's complete declaration as meaning that the 70-week period begins at the rebuilding of the Holy city, Jerusalem and the 69th week ends at the Triumphal entrance of the Anointed One, Jesus Christ, into Jerusalem. That leaves the final week of 7 years for the future. That final week is when a covenant is made with the Anti-Christ in the middle of the seven years *"He will put an end to sacrifice and offering and on a wing of the Temple he will set up an abomination that causes desolation,"* Dan. 9:27. The middle of the 7 years refers to the time between two 3 ½ year-periods. The second being Jacob's trouble, or the 1260 discussed as the Day of the Lord.

Some people believe that this 7-year tribulation will begin and end on a Shemitah year. They would say that 2024-25 could be one of those *beginning* years. This would be a New Beginning of major consequence. Are you depending on your works and charity to get you into Heaven? Here is what Paul says, *"Indeed, I count everything as loss because of the surpassing worth of knowing Christ Jesus my Lord. For his sake, I have suffered the loss of all things and count them as rubbish, in order that I may gain Christ and be found in him, not having a righteousness of my own that comes from the law, but that which comes through faith in Christ, the righteousness from God that depends on faith,"* Php 3:8. The Word states that, *"It is by Grace, through faith that we are saved, it is not of works so that no one can boast."*

Considering Daniel's Prophecy, it spans the panorama of history from the first exile of Israel to the 2nd exile after the Roman dispersion, to the re-unification of the city of Jerusalem in 1967, and to this present age and beyond! It is possible that God's Wheel of prophetic time connects Daniel's Prophecy of 70-weeks to the 50-year special Jubilee which started in 1967. The 70-week prophecy began with the decree from Artaxerxes to restore and rebuild the city of Jerusalem. The "Reunification" of Jerusalem in 1967 may have a connecting role. The concept that Daniel's 7 years parallels or overshadows a Shemitah period is interesting. Is it possible that the 7-year Tribulation period in Revelation represents a 7-year Shemitah period during which the earth is redeemed on the 7th year after the land is laid waste or laid fallow by Apocalyptic war? The Lord's next Coming would then mark the end of that final Shemitah year.

Daniel's 70-week prophecy is a good example of what Prophecy means to the ages. As stated, the prophecy spans generations, centuries, and the Cosmic Crossroad. Sixty-nine of those 70 weeks have already taken place. When one reads the Book of Daniel, not only are you impassioned by the courage and faith of Daniel and his friends, but also about the sovereignty of God and how He has used evil empires and men to accomplish his purpose to protect a remnant and to fulfill prophecy. He used the Roman Empire to provide the Pax Roma so that Paul and others could spread the Gospel throughout the known world, and He used Roman law so that the crucifixion would occur under both Jewish and Gentile authority. His death and resurrection would cover all sin for all time to anyone who believes this and confesses Jesus Christ as Lord.

The final week of Daniel's prophecy could start at any time in the future, but as Daniel states the Anti-Christ must first be revealed and a covenant with Israel must be signed. The Temple itself could be erected in less than a year. This Temple, however, will be a vehicle for Satan and the Anti-Christ to announce their power-grab. Will we know when that covenant is signed? As far as the Anti-Christ we may see him, but will we recognize him as the Anti-Christ? The people who witnessed the life of Jesus for the most part rejected His kingdom, and the leaders and priests did not recognize Him even though they were highly educated and appointed by blood line and tradition to know of His coming. Will today's political leaders make a covenant with the anti- Christ? Will history again repeat itself and will we see men like Herod the Great and a power like Rome's to accomplish His purpose. Will He plan to purify the generations and bring His remnant home?

The number 70 is especially associated with Israel's bondage, exiles, return, and completion of vision and prophecy. As we said earlier the generational numbers 50, 70, and 100 fit perfectly into our period. I do not think this is a coincidence. As mentioned earlier Jerusalem was conquered by the Islamic Ottoman Empire in 1517 and this Islamic force remained in control for 8 Jubilee's or 400 years. This matches the time of Israel's Biblical captivity in Egypt, the 400 years of testing by God's Judges, and the 400 years of silence after the Babylonian exile. As stated, the Turks were finally conquered by the British Empire in 1917.

The growth of the British Empire was accompanied by a great missionary movement into India, China, and other nations. Then one Jubilee later Jerusalem was again "released" from Islamic control in the miraculous 1967 war. So, 8 Jubilees + that Jubilee + our present Jubilee (1967 to 2017) equals 10 Jubilees. We must also remember that it was 70 years ago that the Jews suffered severely under the Holocaust! That generation has almost died off. Will that generation be the last generation? "That generation" is our generation and we have truly little time left! Will God purpose our rebellious generation to be the prophetic generation that fulfills Daniel's 70th week?

There is another remarkably interesting sequence of events in Israel's history related to an ordered series of years and numbers-all pointing to events that affect the nation of Israel and indirectly the world. Note that due to the Hebraic calendar most of these dates span 2 years:

1867-First British Government of Benjamin Disraeli was established
+30 equals…1897
1897- A Zionist conference to find a homeland for the Jews was held.
+20 equals…1917.
1917- England is given a Mandate over Jerusalem and Palestine.
+30 equals…1947.
1947- A special UN conference to find a homeland for the Jews.
+20 equals…1967.

1967- Israel captures the West Bank reunifying Jerusalem.

+30 equals…1997.

1997-The Gaza strip is taken over by Hamas, settlers removed.

+20 equals…2017.

2017- 2021…Now what? What does God have planned for Israel?

The time from 1867 to 2017 adds up to 150 years or 3 Jubilee periods. Each group of 2 dates of significant events adds up to 50 years or one Jubilee. This is a remarkable sequence of events relating to Israel and it points to an increase in activity related to the security and integrity of the land given by God to His People.

Many students of prophecy believe that history shows any nation that interferes with the Promise that God made concerning the land He gave Abraham, have paid a price in some way or another. God's covenant given to Abraham, Isaac, and Jacob, is stated here: *"I will establish my covenant between me and you, and your offspring after you throughout their generations, for an everlasting covenant, to be God to you and to your offspring after you,"* Genesis 17:7. With these sequenced dates, one can grasp that maybe God has purposed a series of historic events to point us to His Coming. This would be the next 7 year "step" in God's stepwise timeline of Jubilees.

In 1867 the author Mark Twain traveled to where Israel is today, describing the land as "barren," "dull of color," and "a wasteland." He was distressed when he could not find a tree to sit under not even a fig tree. God was going to use Twain's declaration in a big way, putting an end to Israel's curse. Israel would no longer stay a wasteland. God would now bless both Israel and England. The amazing victories in 3 sequenced Jubilee dates changed everything. Here are some other notable headlines for the 1st date: 1) In 1867, dynamite was discovered by Nobel, and we know how the Nobel Peace prize played a role in the approaching WWI in Israel. 2) 1867, the British governance of Benjamin Disraeli was established which led to an all-Jewish military unit that would serve the British in 1917 in recapturing the city of Jerusalem and defeat the Ottoman Empire. During this Jubilee of

1917, the Balfour agreement was signed which prepared the way for the establishment of the nation of Israel in 1947-8 and one more Jubilee later the nation of Israel was able to defeat overwhelming forces in the miracle of the 6-Day War.

Unfortunately, Israel is now far from being a spiritual or religious nation. In Haifa, at Mount Carmel where Elijah battled the 900 prophets of Baal there is an ostentatious worship center dedicated to the Gods of the world and run by the Bahai faith. It lights up at night like a mountain size Christmas Tree. It has eleven levels of temples and shrines on the ocean-side of Mount Carmel. The complex of temples and statues is a giant pyramid of idolatry! Israel does not seem to realize that if they do build a temple for sacrifice it will be like this temple – a slap in the face of God who gave His Son as the ultimate sacrifice. Despite their lack of faith God still protects them and favors their mighty military force. But have they forsaken God? Jubilee also embodies Reconciliation.

Next to the Middle East the biggest need for reconciliation in the world is between North and South Korea - who never signed a peace treaty after the Korean war. The blood of the martyrs cries out. It was a Jubilee year when they were massacred, and their land taken. We also see a need for widespread reconciliation here in our own nation. There seems to be a supernatural rise of rebellion and sin in our country. Is this a supernatural preparation for the Anti-Christ, who *"will have no desire for a woman?"* We are in a Roman's Chapter one storm of immorality and perversion where rebellion reigns. Our big box media used to present truth to the world, but now it is under a grand delusion. It acts as both judge and jury determining what is right and wrong in our nation as it defines evil as good and good as evil! These and other lies are reflected throughout the world with increased atrocities, terrorism, apostasy, corruption, starvation, disease, and Christian persecution. An example of what God says about liars and those who follow the lie: *"The one who conquers will have this heritage, and I will be his God and he will be my son. But as for the cowardly, the faithless, the detestable, as for murderers, the sexually immoral, sorcerers, idolaters, and all liars, their portion will be in the lake that burns with fire and sulfur, which is the second death."*

The Serpent said to Eve, *"You will certainly not die."* Satan wants us to believe that God either does not exist or He is impotent and therefore should be doubted. God is alive and He is actively waiting for you or others to come closer to Him, and to follow Him with faith. There is nowhere that God will not go to save you. God is pursuing you with the *"hounds of heaven"* or maybe with the Four Wheels of eyes described in the throne room of heaven? Could this be his "vehicle" to bring Hope and Mercy for you and me?

Despite despair, chaos, and disharmony there is prosperity in America and in Israel. All of which is prophetic as shown in the following verses: Isaiah 60:11, *"Your gates will always stand open, they will never be shut, day or night, so that men may bring the wealth of the nations,"* Isaiah 61:6; *"You will feed on the wealth of nations, and in their riches, you will boast,"* Isaiah 66:12; *"I will extend peace to her like a river, and the wealth of nations like a flooding stream."* I do believe that America is prospering because we do support Israel and because of the prayer of the saints. There is concern that New York City is the "Great Babylon" and that politics in other big cities is opening the door to rebellion and retaliation against both Jews and Christians.

---

Evil forces are trying to undermine our nation and Israel. Iran, China, Russia, and other nations such as North Korea want to see America fall? Will the sign of Revelation 12 which happened on September 23rd portend a silent attack such as digital sabotage or hacking? Read Revelation 12:1 and ask yourself: <u>What is irrational or illogical about this verse?</u> Revelation 12:1 says, *"And there appeared a great sign, a woman adorned by the sun with the moon at her feet and a garland of twelve stars."* I have asked over 200 people this simple question and only one has seen the obvious. Do you see it?

---

The obvious fact is that the appearance of the sun would make the moon, stars, and planets invisible. The word "appears" relates only to the reality that the Sign is there, but it cannot be seen. This is also true of the supernatural. The supernatural exists, but we cannot see it. We cannot see the supernatural forces that are fighting against us or for us. Nor can we see certain natural events like an earthquake, wind, or a virus epidemic. We see increased terrorism, lies, perversion and worldwide uncertainty. We should all keep in prayer asking God for His Mercy in defeating this cloud of evil that is spreading at every level and sector in society. The invisible war is in full throttle caused by both the natural and supernatural agents.

God says, "*Call out to me and I will answer you and show you great and mighty things that you do not know.*" Many call Jeremiah 33:3, God's phone number. I call it God's lifeline of salvation and friendship. This is a reminder that we should not call out His name in vain or in a cuss word, as often happens with a spiritually blind individual. The irony is that even a casual curse may be a curse on oneself. This widespread use of "curse words" or using His name in vain, seems only to confirm who the real God is in this End Time. I hope that this book will be a temporary "Road Map" for those of you who have your *eyes wide open* until you discover God. One should not listen to, nor obey anyone in a fringe religion, cult, or *works based faith* that claims Jesus is an angel or a created being.

This updated version was written to correct syntax and clarify the message since I had little time to edit before the great American Solar Eclipse happened. God had put in my heart that big storms would come soon after and they did. Hurricane Harvey did a tremendous damage to Texas and was the most destructive hurricane in recent American history. Months later both Florida and Puerto Rico were hit by very violent hurricanes.

God wants everyone to know Him and His real name for He says, "*If you ask for anything in my Name, it will be done.*" In the Burning Bush God called himself "I AM THAT I AM" which defines Him as being infinite and timeless. He knew you before you were born and invites you to dine with him. He seeks you in a still place as you open a Bible or book from the Bible. I only discovered God after many years of failed self-pursuit. Finally, in desperation I surrendered my will. I asked Him to take over my life and everything in my life including my dreams and all my desires! I had nothing to lose as I saw my life was spiraling out of control. God answered and changed my life giving me purpose and a real identity.

Do you really know who you are? Do you know whose you are? Do you realize that God knew you before you were born? Do you realize that He planned for you to born in this time and age? *"Faith cometh by hearing and hearing by the Word of God,"* Heb. 11:1. *"If we confess our sins, He is faithful and just to forgive our sins!"* I John 1:9.

Romans 10:12-13: *"For there is no difference between Jew and Gentile—the same Lord is Lord of all and richly blesses all who call on him, for, 'Everyone who calls on the name of the Lord will be saved.'"*

# CHAPTER FIVE

# The Heavenly Wheels, Converging Testimonies, and The Rabbi

When we explore the fall and rise of empires in history it testifies how well God has orchestrated His Plan for us and for Israel. He chose the smallest of all nations to impact the greatest empires. He humbled the greatest empires with wars that were dictated by weather and events that He directed. He spoke to men and women most of whom we call prophets so the world and Israel would see His handiwork. He spoke to teenagers and old men in dreams or visions. These events and people were recorded in His Word as a testimony of God's Grace and Mercy to direct kings, overthrow pagan nations, save people, and forewarn the meek as He changed their mind, heart, and actions. In the Wilderness He gave the wandering nation of Israel instructions to encamp in a Cross formation. That must have been a glorious site at night from heaven's view. They moved their cross-shaped encampment for 40 years in the wilderness. Are you willing to carry the cross in difficult times? God was purifying the nation just as he wants to purify us and build up our spiritual muscles. Go to Figure 8.

In Heaven, the brilliant Wheels are either part of or next to the Cherubim in the throne room. We have explored a few meanings or purposes of these *Spiritual Wheels*. The Bible does not define their purpose nor function, but it does describe them in 2 different passages:

1) Daniel 7:9 states, *"As I looked, thrones were placed, and the Ancient of Days took his seat; his clothing was white as snow, and the hair of his head like pure wool; his throne was fiery flames; its wheels were burning fire."* 2) Ezekiel 1:15-16, states, *"Now as I looked at the living creatures, I saw a wheel on the earth beside the living creatures, one for each of the four of them. As for the appearance of the wheels and their construction: their appearance was like the gleaming of beryl. And the four had the same likeness, their appearance and construction being as it were a wheel within a wheel."* In the book of Daniel, they are described as *"Burning Fire,"* and in Ezekiel that of *"gleaming Beryl"* and as a wheel within a wheel. This is much like a wheel that is spinning so fast with spokes that it appears to go backwards or is it multiple wheels spinning like a gyroscope? In the book of Revelation there are no wheels. Has the function of the wheels and eyes been taken over by the Lamb of God with 7 eyes - meaning total Omniscience? *"The eyes of the Lord are in every place, observing both the good and the evil,"* Proverbs 15:3.

There is another series of passages in Revelation that correlate some of what is seen in the throne room. Now however, the Lord Jesus Christ has been Glorified and He appears as a Lamb with 7 eyes: *"And between the throne and the four living creatures and among the elders I saw a Lamb standing, as though it had been slain, with seven horns and with seven eyes present, but the seven spirits of God sent out into all the earth,"* Rev 5:6. The Four Living Creatures are still present butthe wheels are not described. Why is that? Maybe it is because the focus is on the Lamb who is the Lion of the tribe of Judah and the Root of David. The whole scene changes when the Lamb opens the scroll and every elder and creature bow and worship the Lamb. They sing:

*"Worthy are you to take the scroll and to open its seals, for you were slain, and by your blood you ransomed people for God from every tribe and language and people and nation,"* Rev 5:9. Then the Lamb opens each seal, and the Living Creatures dispense the Horses of the Apocalypses, one-by-one as John watches. Have those horses been released? Many believe so, but I do not, for I think they will all happen quickly with the great earthquake and the 6th Seal coming right behind them. Then comes a period of silence before the Trumpets sound.

This is what God wants us to do now: 1) Pray; 2) Study His Word; 3) Evaluate our lifestyle, thoughts, and desires; 4) Weigh everything in the balance of eternity; 5) and make the changes that are necessary to bring ourselves into fellowship with God. In this way, we can commit to persevering in the Truth, growing in Faith, and acting as an Ambassador for Jesus Christ.

A good question to ask yourself is what is more important in the light of eternity, your eyesight, or your soul? Our eyes are the window to the soul and His eyes can see through them *as they go to and from throughout the earth seeking those who love him and who are called according to His purpose."* II Chron. 16:9. Job said, *"I have made a covenant with my eyes."* Have you made a covenant with your eyes?

Many people are familiar with story of Rabbi Yitzhak Kaduri, a renowned Mizrahi Haredi Rabbi and Kabbalist who devoted his life to Torah study and prayer on behalf of the Jewish people. He allegedly wrote the name of the Messiah on a small note in 2005, on the Day of Atonement and requested that it would remain sealed until his death. He had just given a message in his synagogue on Yom Kippur teaching how to recognize the Messiah! Afterwards he told his students that he met the Messiah. When he died at the age of 108, in 2006, the name was revealed as that of "Jehoshua" or "Yeshua." His son tried to deny this revelation, and it is believed that the son did this to preserve his father's legacy - and his own.

There are many other rabbis in Israel and Jerusalem that are receiving the Messianic message that Jesus Christ may well have been the One God Promised. God seems to be purposing the conversion of many Jews and rabbis and many in Islam. Running parallel to these Judaic revelations is the Vatican Revelation of the 10 last Popes given to St. Malachy who was canonized as the first Irish Saint in the Catholic Church by Pope Clement III in 1190 AD. Pope Francis would be this Last Pope, or the 10th Pope called the *Black Pope* of the Jesuit Order.

There are many Islamists and others in the Middle East who are believing in Jesus Christ. These conversions are drawing a lot of attention and helping to open doors in areas that had only closed doors before. As in Jeremiah 49:36-39, the refugee *"Elamites"* are coming to faith in Jesus Christ. *"And I will bring upon Elam the four winds from the four quarters of heaven. And I will scatter them to all those winds, and there shall be no nation to which those driven out of Elam shall not come." "But in the latter days I will restore the fortunes of Elam, declares the LORD."* Jeremiah 49:39.

Another reputed Rabbi, Judah Ben Samuel, has been making the online news because of a prophecy that he wrote in the Middle Ages a few years before his death in 1217. Ludwig Schneider, an acclaimed Jewish writer who has written for Israeli magazines and has done extensive studies on Hebraic culture and history, says that Ben Samuel predicted the Ottoman Empire (or some tribal empire) would conquer Jerusalem and hold onto it for 400 years or 8 Jubilees. Ben Judah predicted that a timeline of 10 Jubilees total would be commissioned by God for Israel. That happened in 1517, or 300 years after Ben Samuel's death. The Ottomans held on until British defeated them in 1917 exactly 8 Jubilees later! The Rabbi also prophesied that during the ninth Jubilee Jerusalem would be a *no-man's land.* That happened from 1917 to 1967.

The League of Nations wrote a Mandate for the British concerning that "scrubby" piece of land which "belonged" to no nation until Israel became a nation in 1947-48. Even after the war of 1948-49, Jerusalem was still divided by a strip of land running right through the heart of the city, with Jordan controlling the eastern part of the city and Israel controlling the western part of the city. That strip of land was called *"no-man's land"* by both the Israelis and the Jordanians. The strip was removed in 1967 when Jerusalem was reunified in the 1967 Six Day War which was a Jubilee Year!

We know the 9th Jubilee period ended on Rosh Hashanah Oct.5, 1967. The city of Jerusalem had already been liberated earlier in the summer. Ben Judah wrote, *"Then in the ninth Jubilee it will once again come back into the possession of the Jewish nation which would signify the beginning of the Messianic end time."* So, from this statement the *"Messianic End Times"* that he predicted would begin on Rosh Hashanah, Oct 5, 1967, and extend to Rosh Hashanah in 2016. What was supposed to happen during this Messianic End Time? We are now well into this culmination of the Messianic End Time. So now what? Does this suggest a revival in Israel?

I believe that the *"Messianic End Time"* was and is part of the Great Commission which reached out and brought the Gospel to the remaining tribes and nations throughout the world. With radio, television, the Internet, and cell phones, I do believe that we have now reached those remote tribes. We have fulfilled what Jesus commanded, *"And this gospel of the kingdom will be preached in the whole world as a testimony to all nations, and then the end will come."* The prophecy that Jesus spoke would fit right in with Ben Samuel's End Time prophecy. During this period, we have also defeated many evil powers and made Israel a nation to be admired. Many Jews have become Christians and many missions and ministries have been established in Israel.

Israel in many ways has become a good neighbor that God wanted them to be. But they have forsaken God in many ways including through their lust for pornography and perversion. They are a self-determined people often forgetting to give God the Glory. And as the name Jacob implies, they are a stubborn lot wrestling with God. As stated earlier, Israel has allowed the Bahai faith to build multi-level pagan worship center dedicated to the gods of the world on the very mountain that Elijah defeated the evil paganism of his time. This brings up what is obvious, that history seems to move in cycles or circles. This is true as stated earlier, because a clock or wheel is a circle and the Jubilee years, and the generations repeat themselves easily in sets of time. Because generational periods and Jubilee years carry God's judgment, events will follow a pattern in time. Likewise, the Fibonacci sequence often repeats itself in both the stock market and in the exchange market. Both are a measure of the economic pulse.

The testimony of 15-year -old Jewish national in Israel named *Natan*, who died for 15 minutes and then came back to life is very amazing! The Messiah gave him a message for his rabbi. He told his rabbi that "*Mashiach*" is the one known throughout the world and that "Mashiach" had a special message for him and others: "*Israel would have to fight a big war and would win for 2 days then begin to lose!*" He said that "Mashiach" would then save Israel by standing on the Mount of Olives (he used the Jewish name of the mountain) and then the mountain would split in two. He gave a lot of information that sounded like the book of Revelation - which as a young orthodox Jew would be outside his knowledge base. His parents told the rabbi not to make any of this information public, but ignoring the parents, the rabbi videotaped the whole testimony and then published it on You Tube!

We are blessed to have the evidence of the Dead Sea Scrolls that were found in 1947. One of these ancient perfectly copied books was the prophetic book of Isaiah. Isaiah wrote this over 750 years before Jesus Christ and the Crucifixion: "*Surely he has borne our sufferings and carried our sorrows; yet we considered him stricken, and struck down by God and afflicted. But he was wounded for our sins, and he was crushed for our iniquities, and the punishment that made us whole was upon him, and by his bruises we are healed. All we like sheep have gone astray, we have turned, each of us, to his own way; and the LORD has laid on him the iniquity of us all. He was oppressed and he was afflicted, yet he didn't open his mouth; like a lamb that is led to the slaughter, as a sheep that before its shearers is silent, so he did not open his mouth,*" Isaiah, 53:4-6. This is almost a perfect description of what Jesus Christ, a Jew, and the Lamb of God, went through at the hands of the Romans before His death and Resurrection.

Another Dead Sea Scroll book uncovered whose scripture did not delineate from scrolls printed over 200 years later was the book of <u>Daniel</u>. This is proof that the detailed prophetic events in <u>Daniel</u> were a true record of his life and that the prophecies happened as the original text indicated. Chapter 11 of <u>Daniel</u> runs like a detailed history book and just proves that God is orchestrating marriages, wars defeats, and the methods of death. Over 350 Prophecies on the "birth of the child" or the 1st Coming of Jesus Christ happened as predicted by the many prophets in the Bible. The chances of all those prophecies being fulfilled in a random way is a number so big that just to write it out would go to the moon and back! This is the testimony of God's Sovereignty and the accuracy and holiness of the writings of the Prophets who recorded God's message for us. These testimonies are a witness to God's Word so that we can believe. This is just a small part of the Testimony of the Prophets and the Dead Sea Scrolls Jerusalem itself is one of the best testimonies of God's eternal Glory. Israel has survived multiple partial destructions by great empires and was then resurrected by God's Grace and Mercy.

Jerusalem has been or will be recreated 5 times. 1) It was a city controlled by the Jebusites when David discovered it and may have been God's seat at the time of Abraham. Melchizedek, which means "King of Righteousness," was the King and Priest of Salem which means Peace. 2) Destroyed by the Babylonians and rebuilt by Ezra, Nehemiah, and others. 3) Destroyed by the Romans and rebuilt by Crusaders and Sultans and then by Israel. 4) Prophecy suggests that it will be destroyed by the war against the Anti-Christ and rebuilt by the Saints and Jesus Christ. Water will pour from its foundation rock as the inhabitants f lee eastward towards the Mount of Olives which has split in two. 5) Replaced with the New Jerusalem which descends from heaven. Note that we are presently in the midst or middle of this special timeline. This is just a small part of the Testimony of God's

Holy City. *"It is good to sing praise to our God, and it is fitting to sing glorious praise. The LORD rebuilds Jerusalem; he gathers the outcasts of Israel. He heals the brokenhearted, binding up their injuries. He keeps track of the number of stars, assigning names to all of them. Our Lord is great, and rich in power; his understanding has no limitation,"* (Psalm 147:1-5).

We started these Testimonials with the Apostle Peter in Chapter 4 and will continue with the example that he sets for us all. He was one of the first to call Jesus, *"Lord"* and then to call him, *"the Son of the Living God."* His strong and bold approach was a gift designed to break down barriers and draw people to Jesus Christ. His brother Andrew brought Jesus to him and from that point on his life would go from catching fish to fishing in the sea for the world's most stubborn people. Peter was just the person for the job. When Peter saw that Jesus could command fish, he was hooked by a supernatural passion to the Son of God; and soon he would discover that even the wind and storms of life were under His command. In the storm Peter asked permission to come to Jesus. He was the only one willing to take the risk in the middle of a storm. This ability or impulse would lead him to challenge even the mighty Sanhedrin, where this simple fisherman would give God's sermon of the century.

Of course, Peter was the first to realize that Jesus was indeed the promised Messiah and the first to be commissioned by Jesus Christ, to be a rock upon which the church would rest. Ironically, he was the only one that Jesus called *"Satan."* Therefore, many draw a conclusion that Satan's lie which had temporarily blinded Peter might be a lie that would blind the church in the future producing a false prophet and the Anti-Christ's right-hand man. Peter, however, did not let mistakes define him. He let Jesus mold greatness in him. At the crucifixion, even though God let him temporarily fall back on his fears, Peter did not seek pity, nor let fear consume him. God was shaping and purifying him for the test of fire, as He will test us. This fire would not come from the world, but from God in the form of the Holy Spirit and from the refining fire of God's tailor designed wilderness experience. Nothing would stop Peter now except the walk into eternity.

Peter did not fall into apathy nor indifference. He knew that God had a purpose and a plan for him - just as He has for us. Although Peter pulled out the sword, he would eventually rest on the Lord. And that is what Jesus wants us to do as He beckons, *"Come to Me, all you who labor and are heavy laden and I will give you rest. Take my yoke upon you, and learn from Me, for I am gentle and lowly in heart, and you will find rest for your souls. For My yoke is easy and My burden is light,"* Matthew 11:28-30. We can learn from Peter to not to let defeat and fear define us. This may be why God instituted the Feast Days of repentance, ingathering and new beginnings. This was an eternal reminder to Israel and to us that when we fail, we can come to him with a contrite heart and leave with a renewed Spirit.

God desires a relationship with us so that we can see and hear the Truth that transforms. He wants us to learn the value of forgiveness, just as He sent His Son to die for us. Look what the brash fisherman, Peter, turned into. He ran into the empty tomb, led the early church, and gave strength to all around him. Then he wrote some of the most inspiring sound bites and passages in the Word of God. He became a team leader with uncommon leadership skills. That is what God wants for us in trying times. The time of darkness will be a test for us and the church, and an opportunity to be a light on a hill.

This is and will be a time for everyone to be a *Rock* and a *Light* in his neighborhood, just as God designed Israel to be the good neighbor to all nations. Follow Peter's advice, *"For this very reason, giving all diligence, add to your faith virtue, to virtue knowledge, to knowledge self-control, to self-control perseverance, to perseverance godliness, to godliness brotherly kindness, and to brotherly kindness love. For if these things are yours, and abound, you will be neither barren nor unfruitful in the knowledge of our Lord Jesus Christ."* Then Peter goes on to say, *"If you do these things, you will never stumble,"* II Peter 1:5- 8,10.

Do not let the enemy invade your life! The Truth of Bible Prophecy and what I am sharing here is the very hope of the church in this approaching end time scenario. In the Olivet discourse, Jesus commands, *"And the Gospel of the kingdom will be preached to the whole world."* Then in the next breath he speaks of the *"Abomination of desolation, spoken by Daniel the prophet, standing in the Holy place."* We are commissioned as Peter was to persevere in godliness with diligence in sharing the faith to all those around us. This is not just living a good life or being a good example, no by all means, it is an active sharing and exchange of the Gospel message.

Mark 8:34-37: *"Then he called the crowd to him along with his disciples and said: 'If anyone would come after me, he must deny himself and take up his cross and follow me. For whoever wants to save his life will lose it, but whoever loses his life for me and for the gospel will save it. What good is it for a man to gain the whole world, yet forfeit his soul? Or what can a man give in exchange for his soul?"*

We can see that prophecies are being fulfilled as I write this. The Testimony of current events and history is one of the best signs of impending economic problems, war, or some natural disasters. People act like horses with blinders on, going their merry way while the national debt balloons, morality collapses, lies multiply, addiction spirals out of control, and ethics are ignored! Our spiritual decay, the Turkish dictatorship, China's aggression, droughts in Africa, the villainy of North Korea, and the UN betrayal to Israel are all pieces in the prophetic puzzle.

We may not be kings, nor Presidents, but we are God's ambassadors, and we must not be ashamed of the Gospel. We can make a difference. Mark 8:38 *"If anyone is ashamed of me and my words in this adulterous and sinful generation, the Son of Man will be ashamed of him when he comes with the holy angels in his Father's glory."* At the Great White Throne judgment Jesus Christ will play back a person's life and this will heap shame on those who have shammed him. He will open the books and they will be stunned. Notice that it often takes a major disaster to get the attention of the world. This is the condition of the heart in our society. People seem embarrassed to give credit to Jesus Christ or speak of him in an uplifting thoughtful way; much less share the Gospel or pray for someone.

It seems like the media glorifies the lie for its own purposes. The most advanced and powerful nation in the world is being made to look like a "banana republic!" During a mission trip to Southern Africa and found that most people receive their news from CNN, yet they are critical of its accuracy. Never in history has our media been so disrespected and unprofessional. Lies are being told everywhere and to everyone throughout the world. It is not surprising that the *"Flat Earth Society"* argues that we live on a flat earth? After all, lies are so pervasive that they have now become an epidemic and a *"sign of the times."* Likewise, there is a worldwide attempt to boycott Israel. The Dragon's desire is to push Israel into the sea. Jesus called Satan, *"The Father of Lies."* Apparently, few of these leaders and diplomats have read the Bible, nor other historical books that reveal ancient land deeds that record Israel's right to the land.

*"But for the cowardly and unbelieving and abominable and murderers and immoral persons and sorcerers and idolaters and all liars, their part will be in the lake that burns with fire and brimstone, which is the second death,"* Rev. 21:8.

*"There are six things that the Lord hates, seven that are an abomination to him: haughty eyes, a lying tongue, and hands that shed innocent blood, a heart that devises wicked plans, feet that make haste to run to evil, a false witness who breathes out lies."* Prov. 6:16.

The following passages from the Bible are a Testimony from God to help us understand our prophetic time: *"You are of your father the devil, and your will is to do your father's desires. He was a murderer from the beginning, and does not stand in the truth, because there is no truth in him. When he lies, he speaks out of his own character, for he is a liar and the father of lies,"* John 8:44. Jesus Christ states, *"But concerning that day and hour no one knows, not even the angels of heaven, nor the Son, but the Father only. For as were the days of Noah, so will be the coming of the Son of Man. For as in those days before the flood they were eating and drinking, marrying and giving in marriage, until the day when Noah entered the ark, and they were unaware until the flood came and swept them all away, so will be the coming of the Son of Man. Then two men will be in the field; one will be taken and one left. Two women will be grinding at the mill; one will be taken and one left,"* Matthew 24:36. Are you ready for tribulation? Most will not be ready for the rapture nor the tribulation. All scripture from the Word of God is living and active penetrating to ascertain the desires of the heart.

Do the *"Eyes of God"* in heaven connect with the Word of God as it pierces the heart of man? Is it possible that God sees all that happens and is actively fulfilling prophecy while encouraging and helping mankind discover Truth, forgiveness, and humility? God wants us to turn to him and depend on him with a contrite heart and a renewed spirit. He wants to separate us from the world like He did for Moses and Noah. He may want us to separate from an evil world: God led Paul into the wilderness for 3 years to prepare for his ministry; showed Elijah a quiet place at the brook Cherith for his preparation; and hid the early church as it spread throughout the nations and regions.

*"The sacrifices of God are a broken spirit; a broken and contrite heart, O God, you will not despise."* (Psalm 51:17) We should also take special note of all the Trump signposts and testimonies - such as his inauguration happening when he was 70-years and 7 months and 7 days old = 777. His inauguration happened on the 21st day of 2017, and Trump was born 700 days before Israel returned as a nation on May 14, 1948. Also, Kim Clements declared in 2007 that Donald Trump would be God's Trumpet. God gifted Kim with not only a powerful ability to preach, but also with a melodic voice and a beautiful talent with piano. He was a modern-day prophet challenging the world system on stage.

Kim declared, *"Trump will be God's Trumpet"* three times in a loud, triumphant voice! It is interesting that in America the most popular number that is directing us as we commute on our busy freeway system is the 70-mile an hour speed limit. Throughout the scripture and even in the intricacy of His creation, numbers reveal His ordered steps in time and to His Plan for us. After all God put *eternity in our hearts.*

What may not seem important is the testimony of the God's Remnant. God always preserved a remnant. The Ingathering is part of the Feast time after the Day of Atonement, and points to the remnant and to the modern exodus of the Jews back into the land of Israel. A remnant has always survived to preserve Israel and fulfill prophecy. This promise was reported over and over by the prophets. Jeremiah said God would gather them back in the land just before His return (Jeremiah 23:7-8) and restore them to the land of Israel from distant lands (Jeremiah 30:2, 10). Isaiah said God would call them from *"the farthest corners of the earth"* (Isaiah 11:12). King David said, God would gather them from *"north, south, east, and west"* (Psalm 107:3). And Zechariah said, though *"scattered among the nations,"* God will bring his people back into the land of Israel (Zech. 10:9). We see this migration back to Israel occurring right now. Some argue that those promises were fulfilled in the first gathering after the Babylonian captivity. However, there are probably multiple fulfillments. One big one happened when the nation of Israel was established on a barren land that soon flourished with life. As in most prophecies the light shines over many mountain ranges of time and each prophecy may be fulfilled over multiple horizons with each being relevant. Is the pattern expanding to include a final 80-year period signifying the end of the birth pains and the beginning of the Seal Judgments? Will this final prophetic generation usher in the Anti-Christ?

The Testimony of current events and the State of the World is key to the timeline and understanding the Signs of the Time. North Korea and Iran are like two black holes sucking the light from their regions and the earth! Both wish to use nuclear weapons to leverage power against the West. Iran is also the world's biggest sponsor of terrorism with proxy forces all over the world undermining governments and killing both Christians and Jews (including the massive bombing at a Jewish synagogue in Buena Aires, Argentina). Under the arm of Hezbollah, Iran has a worldwide smuggling ring dealing in vehicles, weapons of every kind, explosives, and drugs. What seems most disconcerting is according to the FBI, Hezbollah has active cells throughout the United States. If a war breaks out in the Middle East, it will motivate Iran to activate these proxy forces to destroy our infrastructure and create chaos. Our best weapon is the Sword of the Spirit and Faith: *"For the weapons of our warfare are not of the flesh but have divine power to destroy strongholds,"* 2 Corinthians 10:4.

The New Year of 2018 fell on the Jewish year 5778 and was the year President Trump granted Jerusalem the legal status of capital of Israel. The number 8 implies new beginnings and thus the Jewish Year of 5780 or the year 2020 will expand into a magnification of new beginnings. Likewise, the year 2024-5 will magnify again. The new 7- year Shemitah will be the first to fall in the shadow of New Beginnings. At this point in time, there appears to be a protective covering for both America and Israel. When that veil is removed the enemy which is both spiritual and physical will seek to *"kill, steal, and destroy"* as stated by Jesus who in the same breath promises, *"I came that they might have life, and have it abundantly,"* John 10:10. Are you and your loved one's ready for trials or for the rapture? When I say ready, I mean have you prepared a social-spiritual will for your neighbors, friends, relatives, or workers? More about this later in the next chapter. Will your home be a house of refuge? God has a plan and a promise for you and your family.

God's establishment of the Feast ceremonies is a testament to His desire to teach relationship and surrender. He wants to be Glorified and the Feasts are an instruction book on how to go about it. That is why we must understand that ancient feast days are relevant to today and to prophecy. They are part of Jubilee and therefore part of God's yardstick for measuring earth time and supernatural time. Even though the Holy of Holies no longer exists the Holy Spirit in the heart of believers is real. WE are the Temple. He is measuring the extent of surrender, repentance, and sacrifice in his church and in the world. This is all part of the connection between the *"sword of the Spirit,"* which is the Word of God, and its power to cut into the heart the living and active including the church.

The angelic Creatures and their Wheels may be one way that God is keeping track of everything on this earth. The four wheels may be His vehicle to make sure that Prophecy is fulfilled. They may be protecting all those who are seeking God and keeping watch over new believers. Since time is a factor, could they also be keeping a space-time continuum much like a gyroscope to fulfill prophecy and God's promises?

The World is in turmoil. Mr. Ahok, a Christian man who was a provincial governor in Indonesia was thrown in prison for blasphemy against Islam. All he did was use his political right in an election to ask Muslims to vote for a Christian, but by saying that it was against the Koran. They charged him with blasphemy and put him prison for two years. An increase in Islamic injustice, atrocities, and terrorism is spreading throughout the world. Only God has the answers. We are like sheep gone astray, each to his own way, for the slaughter. A divine light shines in our wilderness and that light is the cross, we must find it quickly for we do not have the 40 years that the "Lost Generation" had 3500 years ago! Satan is trying his best in these last days to fool, seduce, and silence people and nations so that he can destroy them before his great fall.

There is a cloud of irrationality that seems to be pervading the media and the behavior of a lot of people. The open expression of perversion, hate, disrespect to authority, and rebellion is more than just human determination, it is a supernatural darkness that is spreading like a virus. As stated earlier the Bible forewarns of this. Promoting this behavior are blood sports, extreme horror, violent video games, and all kinds of movies. We sell their promotional toys or live action figures to our kids. These practices and behavior are a testimony to the fallen nature of man and of the *"Days of Noah."* The society in Noah's time accused him of being crazy as he built the massive ark on land. It is like the world's media megaphone that ridicules anyone who says the earth is only 6000 years old!

Children and teenagers are less active than ever before, and it may be due to computer games and the social media trend. We are also seeing a tragic increase in teen and adult suicide throughout every class of society. Overlying all this is a dark shadow that is spreading over the church. Jeremiah warned the people, *"Because their shepherds are stupid, they don' t seek the Lord, therefore they don' t prosper, and their flock is scattered,"* Jeremiah 10:21. Churches seem to be more focused on entertainment and agendas than on revival and evangelism. Many spiritual leaders are compromising their convictions and doctrines due to economic pressures from a compromising society. Leaders are afraid to teach the Truth because it might *"create division or discourage those walking in the door."* I was told this when I suggested that our church invite the Institute of Creation Research to teach their view on 6-Day Creation. This non-profit and others like Answers in Genesis offer extensive scientific information to support the historicity of the Book of Genesis and have incredible videos and other teaching materials to show Scientific evidence of the flood and of a young earth. The breakdown in society is the final Testimony in this wheel of time.

It will not take much to create a snowball effect of disorder, anarchy, and unbending fear here in America and elsewhere. We see this happening in many parts of the Middle East, in some parts of Africa, and in North Korea. For instance, the following is a snippet from a newspaper on what happened to a group of Coptic Christians who are now so fearful they want to leave Egypt in mass: *"The terrorists waited on the road like game hunters. Coming their way were three buses, one with Sunday school children. Only three of them survived. Their victims were asked to recite the Islamic declaration of faith before being shot."*

This is a very good reason to turn to God. He is presenting the world with caution signs and alerts foreshadowing this coming *"Cosmic Crossroad!"* Right now, it appears that the spirit of the anti-

Christ is with us. The fact is clear the *"Wheels of Time"* and the Sign of Revelation 12 are pointing to a soon to come epic event. This event is likened to a perfect storm where society breaks down and follows the Anti-Christ into a one-world religion and government.

I believe that the *Last Trump* mentioned in I Corinthians 15:52, is a special moment in time, not related to the Trumpets during Feast of Trumpets, but after the "earthly" trumpets have been blown, God will blow his Mighty Trumpet from heaven as He has done in the past. could happen after another major war in the Middle East or possibly in Asia. Or it could happen at any given moment for a storm of sin and rebellion is already upon us. We will discuss this more in the next chapter. The Great Sign of Revelation 12 happened in the 10 Days of Awe which in the Jubilee year was a special time of Grace when Time was not counted. This happened once every 50 years. It was also a time when the priests were sanctified. Today we are the priests that are sanctified as we share the Gospel and as we prepare for "timeless" heaven.

The 10 years will end on 2027-28 at which time the prophetic 3 ½ years of Daniel's prophecy will commence. God is now purifying the church to strengthen it. It is a time to realize our own weaknesses and failures and then to forgive those who have wronged us.

After the Days of Awe and the Day of Atonement there was a period of gathering of family members to collect the hopes and promises for the new year and the utensils and materials to construct a booth or tabernacle for the Feast of Tabernacles. The feast was a time to come closer to God under the Stars. This is what God desires for His Church and for Israel. He wants us to look up because of His soon Return. Like with the Jewish Feast of Boothes God wants us to bond with His creation, provisions, and family. He wants us to purge sin and enjoy new beginnings in Him.

Both Jew and Gentile were blessed with the prophetic and miraculous "budding" of the nation of Israel and its historical validation. Not only has the nation been a success in every field of science and technology, but it has helped countless nations from South Africa to New Zealand improve and modernize their agribusiness and agrotechnology. They have also come to the aid of dozens of countries affected by earthquakes and other human and natural disaster. God continues to keep His Promise to Israel and when Jesus Christ returns to save the remnant, they will recognize Him as their Savior.

# CHAPTER SIX

# The Cross in the Wilderness
## and Other Answers

First let me emphasize how important the comment section is, especially those detailing the explanation of the Wheels in Ezekiel's vision, detailing the Cross in the Wilderness, the Wheels in Heaven, and the vision that Zechariah had on four spirits. These will unfold as you read through this Chapter.

At the beginning of this book, we saw how the fig tree represents the Nation of Israel which was spiritually dead due to lack of faith. The nation of Israel did not have the faith to depend on God for survival. They did not forgive debts and return the land to the original owners (according to demands of both the Shemitah and the Jubilee). The nation died spiritually early on but in a physical and historical way it died in 70AD, when Rome destroyed the Temple, and the dispersion began. God, however, has not forsaken them. He loves them and has drawn them back as a nation. However, as a nation they have done little to honor him. There is widespread secular behavior in the general population, and they have not been living a righteous life dependent on God.

Right now, God is drawing the Jews to Him and like the remnant during Daniel's time, He will lead the believers to a safe sanctuary near Bosra, Jordan. After the Anti- Christ is defeated, they will return with him to Jerusalem where He will rule during the Millennium. God brings the message back to faith and righteousness and to Jerusalem. Faith calls for reliance on God accompanied by the overcoming of fear, doubt, anger, lust, malice, and the whole myriad of other sins or fleshly desires. Hebrews 11:1 says, *"Faith is the assurance of things hoped for, the evidence of things not seen."* The author continues to testify, *"By faith we understand that the universe was created by the word of God, so that what is seen was not made out of things that are visible, and without faith it is impossible to please him, for whoever would draw near to God must believe that he exists and that he rewards those who seek him."*

*"The LORD will roar from Zion, and shout from Jerusalem. The heavens and the earth will shake, but the LORD will be the refuge of his people, and the strength of the people of Israel."* Joel 3:16.

*"Therefore, if anyone is in Christ, he is a new creation. The old has passed away; behold, the new has come,"* 2Co 5:17. *"It is the glory of God to conceal things, but the glory of kings is to search things out."* (Proverbs 25:2)

Eze 33:5, *"He heard the sound of the trumpet, and took not warning; his blood shall be upon him. But he that taketh warning shall deliver his soul."* A small portion of this book was compiled from information shared among starwatchers, preachers, prophecy advocates, and Bible students asking questions. The great portion, however, was inspiration given by the Holy Spirit linking the stars and the generations to the Word of God, to history, and to the present. I found that information online was often inaccurate, and so have taken care to present the facts.

I pray God will inspire you to keep your mind open to His leading and to write a review on the book's website: CosmicCrossroad. com. While writing this study I contracted Covid-19 but found that it helped isolate me from distractions. It also put me on a healthier diet. It reminded me of when God saved my life the day I became a believer.

Matt. 24:44. *"Therefore you also must be ready, for the Son of Man is coming at an hour you do not expect."* We are to live in the expectation of the sudden arrival of Jesus Christ. The Word says, *"Be alert and self-controlled so that you can pray."*

Jesus warned us that there would be those in the end time that would cry out: *"Lord, Lord, have we not prophesied in Your name, cast out demons in Your name, and done many wonders in Your name?"* Then Jesus said, *"Then I declare to them, 'I never knew you; depart from Me, you who practice lawlessness!'"* Matt. 7:22-23. There are millions of people today who think they are saved, who have a false idea that they can be a Christian and yet live whatever way they wish. They may even attend church on a regular basis, but they do not know God in their hearts and mind. How can a person believe in evolution and still trust in the history of Genesis along with its doctrine of Original Sin.

If you choose evolution, then you have no real reason to believe that Jesus Christ died for your sins. For if you choose evolution, then you do not believe in a literal worldwide flood and God's Covenant and Promise. And if you choose evolution that means you are seeking man's theory over God's Majesty and Sovereignty. Why even claim to be a Christian if you do not believe in His Miracle Power? Seek God with all Your HEART, MIND, and SOUL and you will find Him! Do not be deceived by LIES, for it will be much worse to think you have the truth when you do not. Have faith and be willing to surrender your ego, your will, and your bias to God. Jesus himself said, *"You are either for me or you are against me."* If you believe that Jesus is an angel, then you are against Him. If you just believe that He is a great prophet or teacher, or created being, then you are very much against Him.

2 Cor. 3, *"Godly grief produces a repentance that leads to salvation without regret, whereas worldly grief produces death."*

Questions for you to Answer: 1) Do you think that God had more to say to us when He motivated Kim Clements to yell, *"Trump will be God's Trumpet"* - Maybe God was trying to tell us that Trump will be an instrument of His Grace and Justice? 2) Did President Trump accomplish all that God had planned for him to do? Unfortunately, Trump's brashness and pride got in the way and may have blinded his mission. For his sake God allowed him to lose the election.

If there is a rapture, will only 20 percent or less, of *Christians* be raptured? Will the failure of President Biden generate upheaval, lawlessness, and revolt here in America? Will America see the type of terror attacks seen in Germany, Spain, France, and England? Are you ready for the rapture? - And have you made Jesus Christ the Lord of your life? *"If we confess that Jesus Christ is Lord and believe in our hearts that He rose from the dead then we will be saved!"*

*"And for this cause, God shall send them strong delusion, that they should believe a lie: that they all might be damned who believed not the truth but had pleasure in unrighteousness."* II Thess. 2:11-12.

If you were God and wanted to communicate a warning to all mankind, what would you do? Would you try to communicate a written warning first? Since mankind did not heed God's warnings, what is next? God recreated himself as one of us to feel, touch, and share our pain and tears. He died for us and came back to show us that everything He said and promised was true. Yet many "Christians" fall away into lust, and some have their minds seared and turn away from God.

The *Wheels of Time* have repeated this cycle of repentance to disobedience, righteous pursuit to the glorification of the perverse, from uplifting worship and a relationship with God, to the raising up of the Lie and Deceit. What do you expect God to do? Does He repeat His past attempts to suppress evil and preserve a righteous remnant? Will he then repeat with greater warnings and a greater Sign as He did with the great empires and prophets like Daniel? The Great Sign of Revelation is called a "Great Sign" for a reason, yet both the world system and the Church has ignored it!

He has shown great mercy and patience throughout history. A good example was Nineveh where God sent Jonah to preach, and in due time the evil Empire of Assyria repented. What motivated them to repent? Star charts show that there was a Solar Eclipse that happened right before Jonah arrived. Jesus said to the Pharisees, that to *"an evil generation he would give no sign except the sign of Jonah."* Jonah warned the Ninevites, and they repented after what some believe was a Solar Eclipse. They soon fell back into sin and were conquered by the Babylonians. We have had "Prophets, Preachers and Signs" in our day, yet few have listened and repented.

We are the strongest nation in the world, with power over trade, food supplies, monetary and language control, and natural energy sources; including the most lucrative entertainment and aerospace industries; and countless other God-given resources. God is now beginning to take these away from us for we have taken His gifts and mercy for granted.

We are now the world's greatest producer of junk foods, violent film and games, and idols for worship. Our ideas and ideals are now corrupting the world. We are near the top in perversion, abortion, and gambling. We drive a lot of world's lust, greed, and addictions.

By God's Grace America has a large mission-oriented Church and Christian based charity system that has brought healing of body, soul, and spirit to countless people around the world. We have also been the most consistent supporter and protector of Israel. But time is up. Now the staging begins and that is why Trump is out and Biden is in.

More than ever in history Christians as a group are at the Crossroad of the Promised Return of the Lord coming back in the clouds. What legacy are you leaving behind? Are you sharing the Gospel? Are you preparing your loved ones and others for the rapture, or are you the one that needs to truly repent and believe? Tell your loved ones that Good News, that Jesus Christ accepts and loves them. The God of the Universe has a special Purpose and Plan for them. I have a survival guide in my home for those who fail to make the rapture and it lays out the groundwork of what will happen according to God's well laid out plans. It explains the coming Tribulation, safety concerns, and how to prepare for the Anti-Christ.

God chose a date, September 23, that numerically matches the most popular series of verses in the world - (verses that were placed in my bedroom and in bedrooms of countless children), Psalm 23. The first and only verse that I knew as kid and the one that helped me sleep. Keep verse 3 close to your heart: *"Even though I walk through the valley of the shadow of death, I will fear no evil, for you are with me; your rod and your staff, they comfort me."* Having Jesus Christ in your heart and the Word in your mind will protect you. Understanding the situation and allowing God's Spirit to guide you is of extreme importance during this time. Read blog posts under the categories of "Theology" or "Cults" in ToGodBtheGlory.org. The Lord gave me this website to reach the world for Christ. We had great heroes when I grew up like James Stewart who fought real wars, but the only real Super-hero is Jesus Christ who defeated Satan and his demons, a corrupted religious system supported by a world overflowing with sin and the army of the Anti-Christ. After those 7 years, the Lord establishes His Kingdom on earth. Those who do not believe in a 7-year Tribulation may mistake the Anti-Christ for the Lord.

II Timothy 3:1-5 *"But understand this, that in the last days there will come times of difficulty. For people will be lovers of self, lovers of money, proud, arrogant, abusive, disobedient to their parents, ungrateful, unholy, heartless, unappeasable, slanderous, without self-control, brutal, not loving good, treacherous, reckless, swollen with conceit, lovers of pleasure rather than lovers of God, having the appearance of godliness, but denying its power."*

Concerning these last days Daniel was told by the pre-incarnate Christ, *"But you, Daniel, shut up the words and seal the book, until the time of the end. Many shall run to and fro, and knowledge shall increase."* It seems as if our society is being set up for the "great delusion" that the "Man of sin" will spread over the earth. We already see that with this increasing knowledge there is a loss of God centered knowledge along with irrational behavior, fear, anger, delusional thinking of every kind, slander, riots, chaos, and the blaming of Christians. This reflects both the time of Noah and the time of Nero.

In Zechariah 6:1-8, the following is recorded: *"Then I turned and raised my eyes and looked, and behold, four chariots were coming from between two mountains, and the mountains were mountains of bronze. Leading the first chariot were red horses, with the second chariot black horses, with the third chariot white horses, and with the fourth chariot dappled horses—strong steeds. Then I answered and said to the angel who talked with me, 'What are these, my lord?' And the angel answered and said to me, 'These are four spirits of heaven, who go out from their station before the LORD of all the earth.' The one with the black horses is going to the north country, the white are going after them, and the dappled are going toward the south country. Then the strong steeds went out, eager to go, that they might walk to and fro throughout the earth. And He called to me, and spoke to me, saying, 'See, those who go toward the north country have given rest to My Spirit in the north country.'"*

Horses are fast but chariots are noisy. It makes sense that both white and black horses go to the more populated and warlike northern hemisphere. There War and Peace will shake nations. The dappled horse will imply a source of end-time viral variants in Africa, South Asia, Australia, and South America. The red horses stay put as if protecting the nation of Israel for a time.

One of the last sermons Jesus gave to his disciples included this warning, *"Then will appear in heaven the sign of the Son of Man, and then all the tribes of the earth will mourn, and they will see the Son of Man coming on the clouds of heaven with power and great glory. And he will send out his angels with a loud trumpet call, and they will gather his elect from the four winds, from one end of heaven to the other."* Winds and Spirits are often interchangeable. Is God preparing the world for this trumpet and for His angels to rapture the Church and affect changes on earth that will further activate these chariots?

It seems obvious to me that the banners and most everything designed and orchestrated in the "Wilderness" represents or illustrates the character, nature, and mission of our Savior Jesus Christ. God, in His Majesty and Holiness, designed the events and the materials surrounding the journey and worship of Israel in the wilderness, to Glorify Jesus Christ. Many link the four faces on the Ezekiel Wheels to the four Gospels: man (Luke "*Son of*"), lion (Matthew *lion of Judah*), ox (Mark *the servant*), and eagle (John *the Spirit*). Ezekiel's wheels are described below. Even the four groupings of tribes in wilderness carried banners with these four distinctions! This is described in Numbers 2:2, and the Talmud as twelve tribes of Israel camped under four standards with 3 tribes in each: - Reuben under "man," Dan under "an eagle," Ephraim under the ox (or calf), and Judah under the "lion.

*Ezekiel's vision of the Cherubim and the wheels: The four living creatures had the likeness of man; each had four faces and four wings; each had hoofs like a calf but hands like a man; the four faces were that of man, lion, ox, and eagle; and each had wheels that moved with them. The prophet Ezekiel shares his vision of heaven, "And when the living creatures went, the wheels went by them: and when the living creatures were lifted up from the earth, the wheels were lifted up."*

**FIGURE 8A and 8B**: THE CROSS IN THE WILDERNESS:

My painting illustrates the encampment of the Israelites in the Wilderness. This was part of a paper that I wrote explaining in detail how Jesus Christ was Glorified in the design of the Tabernacle, the Holy implements, the encampment itself and in the symbols used. The graphic art was done in color using about 1000 stones, pieces of glass, and marbles to develop a varied topography of tents showing the different tribes. Note that the tents of Aaron and Moses were right at the entrance to the court of the Tabernacle. The Levites encamped in a rectangular formation around the Tabernacle to protect and maintain the sacred site. All the other tribes are encamped at the 4 compass points adjoining the four sides of the Levite encampment. This automatically creates a cross pattern.

The command God gave was for each tribe to lift their tents and then march out in formation. The cross formation allowed for quick efficient

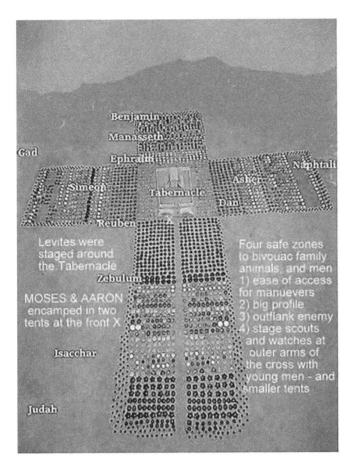

repositioning of men and families to be ready to move quickly in the order of their family groups. The tabernacle was in the center as Judah and his 3 tribes led the camp out into the wilderness. The complete design shows smart military strategy as it would be easy and quick to organize troops into the 4 empty quadrants. It would also be easier to form military lines at each of the 4 arms to out-flank or surround any enemy. With the four arms they could easily post lookouts at each extension to watch for intruders. On a flat horizon a cross gives your enemy the idea that you are much bigger than you really are from every direction. God has everything well planned and orchestrated to Glorify himself and paint a picture of His Promise for us. It is at the that God conquered death and defeated sin for us!

There are signs within the formation of the tribes as they encamped, and in the physical appearance of the Tabernacle which points to both the Cross and the Crucifixion! There are more details under the *Cross and The Wilderness* title at the website: *ToGodBtheGlory.org*. Unfortunately, many biblical scholars without knowledge of desert survival or logical military strategy have erred in their conclusions. The Book of Numbers Chapter 2 is clear in the way the grouping of 13 tribes were arranged. The Cross formation ensures that people had 4 safe zones, each a rectangle between the crosses arms, for bivouacking their families and their animals which would be secure and lit up at night on two sides. All the tribes had to do was march in 4 groups of 3 and then conform their encampment to the outer walls of the Tabernacle and the encamped Levite position. They would set-up tents on North to South and East to West bearing as directed by God. This was easily performed like a marching band. Note the illustration on **Figure 8A & B**.

The 4 empty zones would allow families to exercise, take bathroom breaks, and care for their animals. Two of the 3-tribe groups were of the same general size, one group was extra-small, and Judah's group was extra-large! This creates the tradition cross-look. The so called "dolphin skins" or "badger skins" that some linguists have interpreted for the outer layer of the Tabernacle is another illogical conclusion! The people who first saw the white Arabian Oryx leaping on the horizon amid a water-vapor mirage that obscured their legs must have thought they looked like large white "marine animals" or leaping dolphins! Just as the word "Joshua" has a root word connecting it to the name Jesus, the Jews used a root word indicating a large sea creature. But this does not define it as so. We often use descriptive words that do not define the typology of the animal or plant (for instance a bull shark is not related to a bull, nor is the Tiger shark related to a tiger!)

The outer layer of this 3-layered tent was made of this tough, white Oryx hide and when it dried in the baking sun and wind, it shrank. Note that the Oryx is a large mammal which can be domesticated. This shrinkage opened the ties and bindings and allowed the red dyed rams skin underneath to show through as *red stripes.* By HIS STRIPES WE ARE HEALED! I would not be surprised if the Israelites were given some of these domesticated mammals by the Egyptians for their trip to use as pack animals or just for their milk or meat. It is also possible that the actual hides were prepared prior to the trip as a temporary sun cover, or ground cover, or as a blanket. This thesis was inspired by God as I was designing my award-winning painting entitled "*The Glory of His Majesty and Promise.*" *Yes*! God set the whole encampment up so that He and the angels could see the Plan for Redemption as it played out with this nation which would birth the Messiah. Otherwise, why would God have commanded that the middle layer of ram's skin be Dyed Red? The top bleached hide reminds us that he washes our sin away white as snow. It makes total sense that the four faces on the standards represent the character and Glory as embodied by Jesus Christ. The answers came after a lot of Bible study and mental imagery to create an accurate painting.

Persistent study is how the Magi were able to discover the Savior. God gave us imaginations and creativity so we can understand the design of the interior and exterior of the Holy Tabernacle. It too had the shape and design of the cross. Unfortunately, guides and leaders of the past failed to realize that the "offspring of the woman" would be a suffering Messiah. They could not comprehend that "*God gave his one and only Son, that whoever believes in Him, shall not perish but have eternal life,*" John 3:16. So why has so much misinformation persisted? Is it because of the pride and prejudice of many ego-driven scholars?

Are we as believers going to continue to pay the penalty of not knowing the full extent of His intimacy? God offers us many beautiful images and signs to show how much He loves us. He used banners and elaborate designs to draw his nation to him— it is amazing how MUCH GOD CARES FOR US? Despite all the documents presented by people like Dr. Moller to the seminaries and seminary scholars, they have rejected his in-depth studies and the thesis that Mount Sinai is in Arabia and not in Egypt. Ironically, the secular institutions have not. They saw the evidence and logic and deduced that it was the Truth! We must be cautious so that our dogged determination and traditions do not get in the way of an intimate relationship with the Almighty God who wants a fellowship with us.

God is giving us a sign just as He gave the Israelites one concerning reconciliation and a future redemption. They did not know that they were carrying the Cross throughout their wilderness wanderings. The Cross protected them and in the center of the cross was the sacrifice made for the sin, the Tabernacle, and its red stripped skins. Ironically, Jesus whose stripes would end up as sprinkled blood on the real cross, was there in the wilderness with Aaron and Moses as they sprinkled the blood of the red heifer on the Ark of the Covenant. These signs pointing directly to our future redemption. We as corporeal temples of the Holy Spirit are like the nation of Israel in that God is purifying us and teaching us to be courageous as we struggle in our own wilderness of perseverance.

The nation of Israel did not have the Bible like we do, but they did have the Shekinah Glory and other signs and wonders. Those that looked upon the snake on the brass pole were saved, but those who did not perished. Likewise, those who confess with their mouth that Jesus is Lord and believe that he rose from the dead will be saved, but those who do not possess the faith to believe will die eternally. Jesus is the Living Water just as God was in the water that miraculously flowed out of the rock? He is the *Light of Life*, just as the Shekinah Glory protected and guided the nation of Israel as it wandered the darkness. Jesus is the *Bread of Life* just as the manna was a gift from heaven, and Jesus offers us the *Gift of Salvation*. We have already seen that he is the Ultimate sacrifice, being both the High Priest and the King who gave himself for us so that we might live. Like the nation of Israel our sins needed to be purged by blood so that we might attain righteousness. As a new nation being sanctified, they had to carry their cross, and likewise we are sanctified by carrying our cross. They went through a purifying process in the wilderness, and we will have our own wilderness experience to sanctify us.

The cross is the power of God, a sign of the victory Jesus Christ accomplished over the curse of sin and death. The Mosaic Covenant stated that anyone who hung on a tree was a curse. For this reason, the cross is a stumbling block to the Jew. The cross is hated by those who oppose God and *"Christ crucified is foolishness to the world,"* I Cor.1:18. The Sign of the cross has penetrated every society to the point that the earth lives under the shadow of the cross. It is a testimony of God's love and power over darkness and evil and a reminder that Jesus Christ died so that we might have life. It gives hope to those seeking spiritual Truth and an answer to the world's woes, for it represents the promise of redemption and a relationship with God now and into eternity.

Both the Cross and the Crossroad are signs of God's promise. One has the power to transform hearts and tear down walls of fear and insecurity; the other points to His 2nd Coming and the fullness of his Kingdom that awaits all who place their trust in him. The Cross is the power of God for salvation to all who believe in the One Promised, Jesus Christ. The Crossroad involves a sequence of signs and events throughout history that point to His defeat of death on the Cross, His Return for the Church and then His 2nd Coming to Judge the earth.

The enemy which includes the spiritual government of Saudi Arabia and Egypt, is willing to spend billions to spread the expansive lies of Islam all over America and throughout the world to undermine Christianity. The Saudi government will not allow any

Jew or Christian to step foot in Medina, nor Mecca much less share the faith anywhere in their country! Did you know that they along with the government of Egypt are the main source of money to prove and support the lie that Mount Sinai is in Egypt? They do not want us to know the Truth! What is sad is that many of our Bible scholars have fallen for the lie. Hopefully, they will read this book and will change their way.

All the facts including clear evidence from, Google Earth support the obvious; that Mt. Sinai and Mt. Horeb are in Arabia as stated by the Bible. Islam and the world system seek to take us captive by vain philosophies and lies that undercut our faith and our hope. Like the fallacies of evolution, we have allowed this lie to continue. With Google Earth you can see the huge gorge that confined Pharaoh's troops to a narrow area so that the *Shekinah Glory* would completely block their movement. Look for a large white beach head on the 2nd finger of the Red Sea. You will see a huge sand beach peninsula called *Nuweiba* formed from the extensive erosion of sand from this gorge. This erosion also produced a sand bridge that goes completely across this finger of the Red Sea with an average depth of 100 ft. That is the perfect amount of waterpower to kill and destroy Pharaoh's mighty chariot army.

How could the greatest chariot army of its time drown in 10 feet of *Reed Sea* water? As a military general I would have taken my chariots around the mini-lake and met the Israelites on the other side. This foolish concept or fake story has been sold to our children and to us for generations. Pray for insight, a pure heart, and a right Spirit.

The Nuweiba beach area is so big and white that when panning out with Google Earth you can still see it from a satellite view. Along the beach Solomon's pillar still stands and many believe it marked the spot of the crossing. There used to be one on the Saudi side, but it was removed. The evidence is so overwhelming and has been collected in a beautifully illustrated book called, The Exodus Case by Lennart Moller. He was invited by a Saudi Prince to investigate some archeological ruins near *Jabal Al-Lawz*, a mountain that is scorched on top. Even the Saudi's recognize it as the Mountain of the Law. Nearby is a well called Moses 'well. *Dr. Moller* determined that a village that a Saudi discovered was an altar set up by Moses to make sacrifices. It has a road that curves into a platform with 12 pillars. Those pillars were for the 12 non-Levite tribes. The road was not part of a village, it was really a path for the bulls to follow. Sacrificial blood was sprinkled on each pillar. They also found signs of chariot wheels and carriages in the waters 100 feet deep between the two banks.

An account by the leader of a Bedouin tribe from the Red Sea city of Eilat shines an interesting light. He was befriended by a Christian missionary who was having a hard time convincing him and others that the Bible was true. This leader explained that he could not believe a story about a Midianite priest herding sheep in enemy territory 300 miles away in Egypt when there was plenty of grazing land in the land of Midian! Then by accident the Bedouin saw the first verse in Exodus, Chapter 14. The herdsman immediately recognized the ancient name *Pi-HaHiroth* used to name the site of the crossing! The name had been passed down to him through the ages. That name means *"mouth of the gorge"* and that is exactly where it was located: at the mouth of the massive gorge that runs for hundreds of miles to *Nuweiba*! After the leader saw how true the account was, he and his tribe came to a belief and trust in Jesus Christ!

Let us explore Wheels of Time in heaven and on earth. Jesus is God, the *Alpha and the Omega*, the *Beginning, and the End*. Notice that clocks are arranged as wheels and represent Time. Each *Time Wheel* could have two versions: one measuring Gentile or Gregorian time and the other Lunar or Hebraic 6-to-6 Time. There could be wheels for hourly, monthly, seasonal, and celestial Time. It is my thought that the Wheels in heaven represent the omniscient power of God. Since they have eyes that watch over either the entire world or the church. Do they have built in clocks for day, month, and year? As stated earlier the Word of God is living and active and pierces beyond what the eyes can see. Likewise, these wheels with their eyes may be able to pierce beyond the expanse of heaven into the depths of the human heart or maybe into the future. The wheels that I have used to explain the convergence of events and prophecies are manifestations of what God has planned throughout the ages to represent earth time. They illustrate an ordered set of numbers, or a sequenced and orchestrated symphony of signs, with prophetic dates and events.

The "eyes" that Ezekiel sees on these wheels emphasize total multi- dimensional omniscience! God's eyes *"Go to and fro"* throughout the earth looking for *"those who love God and are called according to His Purpose."* I am sure that they can also see what Satan is up to. They are living creatures and we are the living stones. They are connected to living wheels which embody more than just time. They include the past, present, and future and thus may record History and of the testimonies of the ages.

So, we could say that the *Wheels of Omniscience* are also *Wheels of Time*. They are *Living and Active* much in the way that the *Word of God* is. Maybe they reflect God's Word in Heaven as it cuts through sinews here on earth and divides soul from spirit. We are all naked and exposed in the eyes of God - and to the eyes on these Wheels: *"For the word of God is living and active, sharper than any two-edged sword, piercing to the division of soul and of spirit, of joints and of marrow, and discerning the thoughts and intentions of the heart. And no creature is hidden from his sight, but all are naked and exposed to the eyes of him to whom we must give account,"* Hebrews, 4:12-13. We must remain faithful and not be distracted by the world and its temptations. Ephesians, 6:11, *"Put on the whole armor of God, that you may be able to stand against the schemes of the devil."*

This Cosmic Countdown is part of the biblical countdown to the end of time. Do God's Angelic Creatures act as special agents in historical interventions in both Bible and our modern time? They do act on behest of Almighty God who sits on the throne. The Seal Judgments that are yet to happen, are released by these amazing angelic creatures. Some believe that the seals are released quickly, as the blood of the martyrs is counted, and their request is fulfilled. The 6th seal causes massive panic as the leaders, or "*kings of the earth*" realize that God is judging them. They desperately call out to Him, but it is too late. These mighty leaders then lie to the population telling the world that the Christians who disappeared were killed in the chaos of the massive disasters. The media which is already compromised goes along with it. This is when the Anti-Christ consolidates power and oppresses the resistance.

*God's thoughts are not our thoughts, and His ways are not our ways.* With that in mind we should allow God who created the Universe, tell us that He did it in 6 literal days - "*There was evening and there was morning the first day.*" His Word could not be any clearer. With faith God will show you wonders beyond your own dreams. And that my friend is what makes being a scientist and artist so fascinating and wonderful. Your imagination is a gift from God that allows you to see beyond the confines of the dictates, prejudices, and dogma of others. God wants to speak to us through His Word, through the gift of Creativity, and the mind of a dreamer or visionary. Men like Moses and Daniel, and Women like Deborah, and Abigail are examples of great people in the Bible who followed God faithfully. There are also many great leaders today who affect lives in an incredibly good way. Some have inspired me to dig deeper and search the scriptures for Truth. I want to thank Dennis Kavanaugh, and Angie McCutcheon for their encouraging support and advise as the Lord guided me in producing this challenging project.

There is Hope in Jesus Christ and that is what motivates my friend and I on our weekly mission to White Rock Lake. We have been sharing the Gospel along the bike path near the water for over 5 years now. She gives away free books and I give away free Lemonade. The books vary from Children's Bibles and Bible story books to serious books on Apologetics and Creation. It is a joy to pray for people, to share the Gospel, and to teach them the Truth through Apologetics and just science. Being both a doctor and an artist helps to reach the corners of the mind that some people hide in. The Holy Spirit has blessed us with many opportunities to lead desperate people to the Lord. We have had many inspiring conversations that have helped us understand some of the dimensions of darkness and light that we live in. We keep these people in prayer and hope to continue our mission on Sundays at 2:00 PM near the Chapel Hill Road intersection off West Lawther road.

Through this mission I have had the opportunity to talk to and converse with young people of all ages that seem to know more than many adults. The sad thing is our world seems to be turning a lot of adult minds into a mush of apathy, indifference, mythology, fantasy, perversion, and lust. Satan wants to turn us into spiritual zombies, and it will take a large effort on our part to counter his devious intentions. I challenge any-and-all of you to just listen to inspirational Christian music and sermons for a least 30 days and obey God in all that you do. Keep in prayer and give God the Glory and I believe Holy Spirit miracles will happen in your life. And for that reason, I would rather trust the guidance of the Holy Spirit than a dogmatic system of thinking or a wayward science that is corrupted by worldly tradition or agenda- oriented philosophy.

The Apostle Paul said, "*I focus on this one thing: Forgetting the past and looking forward to what lies ahead, I press on to reach the end of the race and receive the heavenly prize for which God, through Christ Jesus, is calling us.*" Philippians 3:13-14.

# CHAPTER SEVEN

# The Perfect Storm

The perfect storm is almost upon us, and many could argue that it is already here. Two of the most Biblically sound governments in the world have recently been overturned: One by a questionable election controlled by quickly made-up election laws and regulations, darkened voting halls, harvested ballots, and questionable ballots tallied after midnight or after evacuation of polling officials under false pretenses. And the other, the nation of Israel, by accusations of bribery that so far have not been proven. Both leaders were highly influential in their respective religious circles and were part of a God inspired change in the legal status of Jerusalem. Together they broke barriers and destroyed the status quo set by ex-Presidents and the world system.

So why did God not keep them in office? Reasons include God's plans to prepare for the perfect storm. Both had pride that may have hindered their testimony and credibility. Both of their nations now have "all-inclusive governments" that cater to an extremely wide spectrum of beliefs including those practicing perverse lifestyles, anti-authority groups like BLM, anti-God sects including Satanism and witchcraft, and those who just hated Netanyahu and/or Trump. Amazingly each has elements that want Palestinians to have more control of the Holy land. Both new governments are more likely to compromise with a "Charismatic World Leader" and may show weaknesses that will invite an outside attacker to invade or assault one of its major allies. It is also possible that God wants to separate or isolate both the Church and the Orthodox Jews in order to draw them closer to Him. Both need help.

The Great Sign of Revelation 12 stands as beacon of Light warning of a coming storm and events that Jesus shared in His timeline of end-time events. Likewise, the Fig Tree parable puzzled scholars through the ages. We have seen that neither seem to fit a chronological order in Christ's narrative. However, both including the Genesis 3:15 curse and Daniel's 70<sup>th</sup> week prophecy, were designed to pop up like bursts of perfect light or lightening in the final countdown to the final hour.

Each is a powerful symbol of what God sees for His Church. The Fig Tree is one of the hardiest fruit-bearing trees - some bearing 3 crops a year. Its deep roots and tough trunk can take drought and heat while providing the perfect shade for the tired and beaten down. Earlier we saw that the 12<sup>th</sup> Chapter in Word is in the center of His will. The number 12 is a complete measure of holiness or time in heaven and earth. We see 12 elders, 12 lampstands, 12 gates, and 12 cakes of bread in the Temple. Jesus chose 12 disciples among the 12 tribes and had 12 full baskets of leftovers after his miracle. There are 12 hours to the day and 12 months to the year.

There are many harbingers of this approaching storm. The winds of war and chaos are growing stronger as leaders like Merkel, Trump, and Netanyahu are replaced by those who are likely easily manipulated. The shackles of mind-control and religious slavery are spreading as nation building and democratic systems faulter. A nest of terrorism is growing in Afghanistan, Africa, and Yemen along with well-organized proxy armies loyal to Iran. And the biggest threat lies within a blinding nuclear rocket race with not only Russia and China but with Iran, North Korea, Pakistan and India. The Eye of Evil is growing darker.

People see and hear about this in the news, yet few perceive the sinister power ready to pull the trigger, when the right moment comes. Beyond ISIS, the Taliban, and Al Quida are dozens of smaller suicidal armies eager to overthrow governments, assassinate leaders, destroy schools, kill Jews and Christians, and some are so demonically directed they seek profit from the rape, kidnapping, and enslavement of children. Over decades those hardened by their masters have formed an invisible army that is bent on the over-throw of all opposing authority. Jesus Christ is the only answer: *"I AM the light of the world…If you follow me, you will not walk in darkness but will have the Light of Life."*

It is easy to see that a Perfect Storm is occurring in the heart of man. God addresses needs for every human: *"Flee sexual immorality. Every sin that a man does is outside the body, but he who commits sexual immorality sins against himself."* I Cor. 6:18. And in Gal. 5:19:-21, God lists the evil: *"Now the works of the flesh are evident, which are: adultery, fornication, uncleanness, lewdness, idolatry, sorcery, hatred, contentions, jealousies, outbursts of wrath, selfish ambitions, dissensions, heresies, envy, murders, drunkenness, revelries, and the like; of which I tell you beforehand, just as I also told you in the time past, that those who practice such things will not inherit the kingdom of God."* God directs each of us, *"Therefore put to death your members which are on the earth: fornication, uncleanness, passion, evil desires, and covetousness, which is idolatry. Because of these things the wrath of God is coming upon the sons of disobedience, in which you yourselves once walked when you lived in them."* Col. 3:5-7.

The perfect storm is for the sons of disobedience who will be given one more chance to seek out redemption in the Savior who offers the Light of Life amid worldwide darkness. Ps. 103:10-13 describes the heart of God: *"He does not treat us as our sins deserve, nor pay us back in full for our wrongs. As high as heaven is over the earth, so strong is his love to those who fear him. And as far as sunrise is from sunset, he has separated us from our sins."* Jesus loves us beyond human logic.

The global pandemic, extreme weather, and sectarian wars have already created a massive refugee problem and a humanitarian crisis that will add to chaos on earth. China is using bribery, extortion and economic leverage to take control of strategic shipping choke points around the world. They produce 5 warships to each one America makes. Foolish politicians gave away technology and secrets to both Russia and China hoping to draw them into the world's peace-loving community. That failed miserably. Dictators Xi and Putin are now awaiting the chance to invade Taiwan, the Baltic states, and Ukraine.

Many other leaders have turned from God and godliness and are using climate and population control to bring in a One-World system that promises to solve every problem. However, their blindness, partisan politics, excessive spending, bloated corruption, and a woke mentality will allow a final dictator to take control. The stage is set for the perfect storm and the ushering in of the anti-Christ. No wonder God is allowing Covid-19, rumors of war, and earthquakes to spread world-wide. He may be using these promised birth pains to save the world from itself. This delay will allow many to find the Truth in Jesus Christ.

It is no coincidence that masking, vaccinations and border controls are making the daily news. This is a worldwide trend towards the control and breakdown of what used to the independent spirit. People are being forced to conform to new forms of compliancy and compromise. This borderless, faceless society is part of the staging for the ultimate deep state. Your name, address, location, and health records whether in the real world or the virtual world will become more and more a part of a global monitoring system designed to know who you are, how well you are, and where you are at any given moment. Science and technology have advanced far enough to be able to implant all the necessary parameters and data into a tiny chip the size of a rice grain.

Masking, vaccinations, and lock downs are just the beginning of a quickly changing world system that will see increased controls in schools, workplaces and the marketplace. Dark powers seek to control human behavior. They have already brainwashed generations of youth to worship science over the Creator. The invisible war began years ago and only broke through like a contagious pox with the redefinition of the family and the reordering of God's sexual order. Since 2017 there was a great increase in lawlessness against any authority and a deep rebellion against God resulting in a generalized spiritual and moral collapse. The Lord will return soon to save the Church, but first she must fight for the sake of the lost by putting on the full armor of God.

*For we are not fighting against flesh-and-blood enemies, but against evil rulers and authorities of the unseen world, against mighty powers in this dark world, and against evil spirits in the heavenly places,* Ephesians 6:12.

Daniel tells of another invisible force which is at work, *"I saw in my vision by night, and behold, the four winds of heaven were stirring up the Great Sea. And four great beasts came up from the sea,"* Daniel 7:2. Those heavenly winds blew in Daniel's time, through much of Israel's history, and are blowing now as a divine harbinger of the approaching final beast. Covid-19 is part of this wind and is why the virus has not gone away. This invisible agent alone has destroyed the tourist industry and kept Christians away from Israel. God is orchestrating events for His purpose. War in the Middle East may be fast approaching, and He has other plans for the Church.

This draws us to one of most significant signs of the time. Israel is the prime target of all kinds of dark forces brewing in the Middle East. In God's eye and in the eye of the Great Dragon of Revelation 12 Jerusalem is the epicenter of the world. Right now, Israel and Jerusalem are not the only targets; the Gulf States which made peace with Israel are more vulnerable. They will be hit first. Billions of dollars of Black-Market money have been funneled through and laundered in Dubai and other skyscraper cities. It includes the blood money from slave markets and the pornography industry. Know that this diabolical movement is wider and deeper in the "civilized" West and is manifested in the celebration of all kinds of aberrant behavior including homosexuality and demon worship. It draws millions of teens and children away from God and blinds their heart and mind. But it cannot be hidden from the eye of God. Judgment is coming soon.

Christians have been a target ever since Jesus warned "*just as they hated me, they will hate you.*" And it is not only because Christians are willing to stand up against abortion, transgender tyranny, illegal immigration, critical race theory, and any dark agenda. There is a visceral element, a spiritual power that hates both Jews and Christians and a crazed liberal media is its mouthpiece. This multi-headed beast welds power against Christians – they convince those who want the freedom to sin that Christians are their biggest obstacle. That is why abortion will continue to be weaponized to a super-high degree against anyone or any authority that comes against it.

In the human element, the Perfect Storm has another powerful Sign: "*Occult brainwashing & Demonic possession.*" Like in a Stockholm Syndrome people have become profoundly captive to evil and the dark forces. Oxford defines this syndrome as "*feelings of trust or affection felt in many cases of kidnapping or hostage-taking by a victim toward a captor.*" God states that we have a choice: to be a captive of sin or to be a captive of righteousness. There is a very powerful invisible undertow pulling and pushing people further and further out into the deep dark waters of the unknown. Many grow fond of the captivity and uncertainty thinking it is a friend. It will, however, suck one down when one least expects it. The intensity of this invasion and captivity is growing and this is ONE BIG reason why the LORD is returning.

Volcanic activity is intensifying and will soon impact greater areas of the world. Just as the winds of the invisible war warn of the coming storm volcanoes like Mount Vesuvius can be a fiery harbinger of the approaching end of Empires. Recent eruptions and earthquakes are impacting the earth now with greater intensity. Presently we have 50 active volcanoes that at any given moment could release lava or gases. And new ones are becoming active at a relatively fast pace. The increased intensity of forest fires and all forms of severe weather are another harbinger.

If you look back, 2017 broke all records for FEMA expenditures and each year thereafter has had its own record fires and winds. The recent Dixie fire in California has finally been put out by a massive storm after it destroyed over a million acres of prime forest land. The birth pains are coming in waves and are presently shaking every part of the earth including far-reaching islands. Are these fearful shakings directed in areas where the darkness dwells? For God speaks from heaven against those dark places of evil and against those who weld the scepter of Satan against the innocent and against his church.

The Apostle Paul does encourage us, "*For I am persuaded that neither death nor life, nor angels nor principalities nor powers, nor things present nor things to come, nor height nor depth, nor any other created thing, shall be able to separate us from the love of God which is in Christ Jesus our LORD*," Roman 8:15-17. God's Love will reach you in the deepest darkest pit and can rescue you from the coming hell on earth, just Ask Him. The Author knows – For the LORD saved him from Hell and made him a new Creation and gave him a new Life. His testimony will be in the sequel to this book.

# CHAPTER EIGHT

# The Final Chapter: To Those Who are Left Behind

The <u>God's Must Be Crazy</u> was a movie that came out when I was in school trying to find myself. And I was indeed lost. This Buster Keaton-like movie came out in 1984 at a perfect time to expose what George Orwell's book, 1984, did not. Big Brother did not happen, instead we had mass transport, mass communication, fast food, fast living, and people always in a hurry to get somewhere! If you remember back in Chapter 12, this was exactly what Daniel was told by the man in white linen. By speeding up the film movie director simulated the chaotic race that our society has been on for decades. He then portrayed the simple life of a *bushman* in the *Serengeti* of South Africa. Life goes to pieces for this bushman when a Coca Cola bottle falls from heaven (from a small plane) and hits him on the head. He takes the bottle back to his village and discovers that everyone has a use for it and wants to have it for themselves. To solve the jealousy and greed problem, he decides to take it to the end of the world to give it back to the gods. He runs into all kinds of trials. Emotions take us down the wrong road, only Jesus can solve the sin problem.

In the meantime, our world is moving like a swarm of crazed ants at higher and higher speeds; often in tight circles of traffic and in slow arduous traffic jams, searching for answers, each on his or her own hurried mission. This contrasts with the simple practical life of the bushman who only kills what he can eat. This is a picture of what has happened in the Timeline of life. We cannot just jump off, but we must find the window to heaven that this bushman was searching for. There actually is a place near the Serengeti called "The Window to Heaven" and it is where the movie was filmed. Like many places in the world, it is a little piece of God's beautiful handiwork. There is also a REAL Way to Heaven and a narrow gate. Jesus says, *"I AM the Way, the Truth, and the Life, and no one comes to the Father except through me."* There is absolute Truth and a *Life* that transforms giving purpose and meaning. There is a Gift that God will give you, an identity that no one can steal, kill, or destroy. Prophecy suggests that at least 2 major events will happen suddenly and maybe simultaneously which will shake the world both physically and mentally! The first is a major earthquake and the 2nd will be the disappearance of many people! This final one is symbolized by the window or the door to heaven.

It is interesting to note that Yellowstone National Park is described as both the Serengeti of America for having the largest open field ecosystem, and one of the most dangerous natural wonders in America. It is the largest semi-active volcano in the world. Some would say it is no longer a volcano, but that depends on how you define a volcano. It is a massive crater having a thin layer of earth's crust with constant vents pouring out boiling mud and water, and whose tectonics show ever increasing earthquakes. Yellowstone in a way symbolizes what is going on in America. We have a social volcano that could erupt at any time and most people seem oblivious. The volcano that I refer to is not just fire, it is likened to a sore in the center of our country.

Yellowstone blew its top centuries ago creating a deep caldera or thinning of the crust! And whether you want to believe it or not, it could erupt. We have a new Solar Eclipse in 2024 that will cross over the center of the Great American Solar Eclipse of 2017 - right over the Madrid fault. Will this be a catalyst for an earthquake? Also 2024-25 will be the end of the 1ˢᵗ Shemita or Shmita of the new century and new Jubilee. This will be election year in America with the forces of darkness aimed at disrupting this extremely important event. A window is opening to God's intervention. It could mark the beginning of the end. Both the Anti-Christ and the two witnesses will be revealed near the end of this period. And Satan will be cast from heaven.

God will act throughout the world in reaction to increased hate poured out on "Christians" and the church by Islam, the media, the cults, and those sold on the perverse. The government and other sources will try to explain this mass disappearance as being part of a global phenomenon, aliens, or just the aftermath of some strange natural disaster. This Divine earthquake will cause massive fires, tsunamis, volcanic eruptions, and darkening of the planet and sun - with the moon turning blood red. Do not listen to the lies of the media but do Look Up. *"Look up! For the Lord drawth nigh!"* I say this not as a momentary solution, but as an attitude that calls one to seek the Savior with all heart, mind, and soul - and to open the Bible and pray. God says, *"Be alert and clear minded so that you can pray!"*

*"Behold, I shew you a mystery; We shall not all sleep, but we shall all be changed, in a moment, in the twinkling of an eye, at the last trump: for the trumpet shall sound, and the dead shall be raised incorruptible, and we shall be changed. For this corruptible must put on incorruption, and this mortal must put on immortality,"* 1 Corinthians 15:51.

*"But if the watchman sees the sword coming and does not blow the trumpet, so that the people are not warned, and the sword comes and takes any one of them, that person is taken away in his iniquity, but his blood I will require at the watchman's hand,"* Ezekiel 33:6.

The "End is Soon" is one sign that best reflects the situation. However, the Lord will return just as He was raised up in the clouds after His resurrection. Acts 1:19, *"They were staring into the sky where*

COSMIC CROSSROAD COUNTDOWN

*he had gone. Suddenly two men wearing white clothes were standing beside them. They said, 'Men from Galilee, why are you standing here looking into the sky? You saw Jesus carried away from you into heaven. He will come back in the same way you saw him go."* There is a rapture and then there is the 2nd Coming when Jesus Christ sets His feet on the Mount of Olives and defeats the armies of the Anti-Christ. Jesus, the King of Kings, will appear to all the surviving Jews and they will say, *"Blessed is he who comes in the name of the Lord,"* Matt. 23:39.

If you are left behind, you will be tested and everything around you will start to disintegrate including social order! There are, however, many places of sanctuary that you will need to find - these include homes, ranches, and retreat areas that Christians have owned and are now abandoned. Since Hollywood has been such a thorn to God's message, I believe that it will come under swift judgment. This is part of the transformation that hands the prophetic clock over to a world leader that will fulfill prophecy. We are seeing so many scenarios of *"Armageddon"* in the movies that it seems as if God is trying to warn us through the minds of men who have been gifted the ability and resources to communicate with the masses. Is it possible that both the Pacific and Atlantic oceans suffer from a surprise asteroid that triggers a massive earthquake and a series of large volcanic eruptions that block the sun and affect worldwide weather?

The Prophet Joel says it best: *"The sun shall be turned into darkness, and the moon into blood, before the great and the terrible day of the LORD come."* Look to Jesus Christ and remember, *"That God so loved the world that He gave his only begotten Son so that no one will perish, but will have eternal life,"* John 3:16. God will select 144,000 righteous Jews to stay behind to teach and preach the Word. There will be two witnesses who perform great miracles, and who will be murdered by the Anti-Christ in front of an international television audience at the Temple Mount.

*"Thy will be done on Earth as it is IN HEAVEN!"* Our Hope is in God. It is by Grace through faith that we are saved - a Free Gift -

so that no one can boast. Yes, that Gift mentioned earlier is Jesus Christ who died so that you may live. There are other mysteries that God has revealed over time and the greatest of these is the church. Understand that the church is not organized religion. The church was a group of men and women who had experienced the greatest miracle of all time.

They were being hunted, yet they relied on the God's direct protection and then on the Holy Spirit. They did not have agendas, marketing tools, high debts, and fears of success. They were God's people, and their purpose was to get the message out to the masses as quickly and accurately as possible. The church has been the voice of God for about the last 2000 years. The church carries the promise and is the fulfillment of His Prophecy. Understand that every human is imperfect, and therefore the church is not perfect. These are humans who make mistakes, and learn from mistakes, and who themselves are trying to convey the Truth of the Word of God.

Has God inspired this book? Many of the ideas were inspired as we shared the Gospel with others. Sharing the Gospel is a blessing, a lesson shaped by the supernatural for only the Holy Spirit can truly convict the heart. The closest that we can come to touching the artery that feeds the soul is to enjoy the *Heart of God* as it pumps Truth into our relationships and conversations. God's Truth is revealed through His Word, and we are the only ones that can do it for Him - the members of His church who were chosen by Him, for Him, and through Him.

As stated, before even though the Temple and the Holy of Holies no longer exist, the Holy Spirit is in the heart of anyone who receives God's Gift. The Spirit is real, and He is measuring the extent of surrender, repentance, release, and sacrifice in His church and in the world. The Bible is the Living Word of God and therefore, think of every word as part of a prayer or a letter to your heart, mind, and soul. There is great power in the Holy Spirit. God said, *"Not by Power, Not by Might, but by my Spirit."* This is not the power that we see in the world, it is a power beyond human origin that is supernatural, and life changing bringing us into a relationship with the True God of the Universe. It is the Power of the Holy Spirit, *"For God did not give us a Spirit of fear, but of power, love and self-control."* Jesus Christ is the Door to Heaven, and he invites us to come in. He is a Strong Tower, for He protects and defends us. He is our Kinsman Redeemer, Savior, and Mighty Counselor. He is the Ancient of Days and the Beginning and the End. We can look to Him to give us a New Beginning and to impart it on those we love.

THE BAD NEWS is: 1.) *"We are all sinners and have fallen short of the Glory of God,"* Romans 3:23. 2.) *"The wages of sin is death, and the gift of God is eternal life through Jesus Christ,"* Romans. 6:23

THE GOOD NEWS is: 3.) *"For God so loved the world, the He gave His only begotten Son, so that everyone who believes in Him, will not perish, but will have eternal life."* John 3:16. 4.) *"But God demonstrates His love in this, while we were still sinners, Christ died for us."* Romans 5:8.

To you who are burdened by the weight of performance and works, God speaks to your soul with this simple Truth: *"For it is by Grace, through faith, that you have been saved, it is a Gift of God, so that no one can boast."* Eph. 6:8-9. Second Corinthians 5:17 says, *"Therefore, if anyone is in Christ, he/she is a new creation the old has passed, and behold, new things have come."* The transformation that happens to our heart and mind after we trust in and surrender to the Lord is beyond explanation. I can remember the fog in my brain leaving as God's Spirit tore down the walls of bad habits, poor thinking, and many fears, anxieties, and bondage. He will wash us as white as snow. This includes our minds, our fears, and dreams.

He truly lifts and carries our burdens and confusion so that we can live with purpose and identity. We indeed become *"New Creations"* with *New Beginnings*. It is a great joy to give God the glory for the writing of a book. What an adventure it is to join God in overcoming obstacles while shining His Light in dark and obscure corners. At one point when losing data, I felt overwhelmed with despair, yet His Grace transformed it into a baptism by fire. He lifts us up all the stronger as His love purges us of fear, frustration, sin, and pride.

The LORD put this Book in my heart months before the *Great American Solar Eclipse.* The Invisible War happened just as the Sign said it would. We now live in a new Paradigm as a result of this worldwide invasion and the lawlessness that followed. God gave 7 major insights to warn us. He put the message in the "Stars," but both the church and the world were blinded by their worldly pursuits. The Sign transpired in a combination of movements in the Sun, Moon and Stars. These Signs included the Solar Eclipse, the 4 Blood Moons, and the Great Sign of Revelation 12. These are all tied together along with the Festivals and Generational markers to forewarn us of events that are Purifying Israel, the Church and those He seeks to draw to Him. The Countdown has been set. God put eternity in our hearts, and soon He will put eternity in our entire being. For updates, you can check out Facebook pages *SOS Save Our Souls* & *Cosmic Crossroad Countdown* and website: *CosmicCrossroad.com*.

The artwork in the photo is called "Jesus Christ the Door to Salvation" which is a mixed media painting. You can see more of my artwork on the blog site ToGodBtheGlory.org. The photo shows me holding my constant companion during the hurry to get this important book out. The experimental painting looks completely different in full color with a 3-D door lit up by a string of LED lights. The 4 Horsemen of the Apocalypse and man's rebellion are portrayed as Jesus Christ and Holy Spirit hold Hell in place while seeding the world with the Word of God. Jesus Christ opens the Door yet the world rebels as the prayers of the saints is sent up to heaven. The mixed media is done on an 8 foot by 4 foot pink board.

The sequel to this book will reveal a surprise combination of events that point to the end-time. It will also detail in depth the 7 insights and the invisible forces responsible for our increased uncertainty and lawlessness. Satan is trying to stop Israel and the Church but *"He who is in us is greater than he who is the world."*

CPSIA information can be obtained
at www.ICGtesting.com
Printed in the USA
LVHW111643260322
714493LV00002B/15